Wealth Unleashed

A Guide To Financial Independence

WEALTH UNLEASHED

First edition. December 14, 2025.

ISBN: 979-8231021369

Written by Juliet Alambo.

Also by Juliet Alambo

Ripples Of Faith

Hearts Of Valor (Ripples Of Faith)

Standalone

The Trouble Makers

Toto Gets Lost

God Is In My Story

The Rebel

Stepping Into God's Promises and Blessings

Deliverance In Christ Jesus

Beyond The Visible

Beauty With Character

Marriage With Purpose

Praying Effectively

Rosy The Lazy Girl

Atito The Foodious Boy

Life O Life

Merry Merry Christmas

Deep Trust In God

God's Grace To Man

Harry Visit's Grandma

Journeying Through Life

Money Matters
How To Have A Perfect Marriage
The Heiress Returns
Wealth Unleashed
Home This Christmas
Secret Sin
The Shivers Beneath
Christmas Healed Heart
The Star Of Christmas

Table of Contents

- ◈ PREFACE 1
- ◈ DEDICATION PAGE 2
- ◈ ACKNOWLEDGEMENTS 3
- ◈ FOREWORD 5
- ◈ Chapter 1 — The Beginning 7
- ◈ Chapter 2 — Mindset 13
- ◈ Chapter 4 — Climbing the Corporate Ladder 24
- ◈ Chapter 5 — Networking 30
- ◈ Chapter 6 — Spending Wisely 37
- ◈ Chapter 7 — Saving With Purpose 43
- ◈ Chapter 8 — Investing 50
- ◈ Chapter 9 — Escaping Debt 58
- ◈ Chapter 10 — Emergency Preparedness 65
- ◈ Chapter 11 — Budgeting 73
- ◈ Chapter 12 — Building Financial Habits 82
- ◈ Chapter 13 — Multiple Income Streams 90
- ◈ Chapter 14 — Breaking Bad Money Habits 100
- ◈ Chapter 15 — Discipline 110
- ◈ Chapter 16 — Health & Wealth 118
- ◈ Chapter 17 — Mentorship & Community 127
- ◈ Chapter 18 — Identity & Self-Belief 134
- ◈ Chapter 19 — Money & Relationships 143
- ◈ Chapter 20 — Entrepreneurship 154
- ◈ Chapter 21 — Long-Term Wealth Strategy 163
- ◈ Chapter 22 — The New You (Final Chapter) 171
- ◈ You Are the New You Now 176
- ◈ Final Page Closing Quote 177

◈ PREFACE

Every journey begins with a single decision — a moment when you realize that the life you want, the peace you crave, and the future you dream of will only arrive if you decide to build it.

This book was born from conversations with real people: **those struggling to make ends meet, those trying to climb the corporate ladder, those starting from zero, those trying to rebuild after setbacks, those seeking clarity, control, and confidence with their money.**

I wrote this book because too many people feel defeated by their financial circumstances. Too many believe that wealth is reserved for a chosen few. Too many carry dreams that slowly suffocate under the weight of fear, confusion, and financial stress.

Financial independence is not about luck. It is not about inheritance. It is not about being born into privilege.

Financial independence is built.It is learned.It is shaped.It is created through mindset, discipline, vision, and practical steps applied over time.

This book is your guide — simple, relatable, practical, and deeply human. It speaks to the person who is tired of struggling... the person who is ready to take responsibility...the person who wants more...the person who believes they were meant for better.

As you turn these pages, I invite you to reflect, to learn, to act, and most importantly, to believe.

Your financial future is not a mystery — it is a masterpiece waiting for your hand.

◈ DEDICATION PAGE

To everyone who has ever looked at their bank account and felt fear...

To the dreamers who were told they would never rise...

To the parents fighting silently to build stability for their children...

To the young people trying to find their way in a world that moves too fast...

To the workers who give their all yet feel unseen...

To the unemployed who haven't lost hope...

To the believers who know they are meant for more...

This book is for you.

May it strengthen your courage, sharpen your vision,
and remind you that your financial future is still yours to shape.

—-

ACKNOWLEDGEMENTS

This book was not written in isolation; it is the result of countless conversations, observations, and shared experiences.

I want to thank the individuals who opened their hearts and shared their financial struggles, victories, fears, and dreams. Your stories gave this book its humanity, its relevance, and its purpose.

To the mentors, financial experts, and everyday heroes who taught me that money is not just numbers — it is psychology, discipline, and identity — thank you for your wisdom.

To the friends and family members who encouraged this work, who believed that it would touch lives, and who reminded me that knowledge becomes powerful only when shared — I am grateful.

And to every reader who picks up this book with an open mind and a willing heart:

thank you.

Your journey is the reason these pages exist.

—-

◈ FOREWORD

Financial independence is one of the most misunderstood concepts of our time.

Many people assume it requires extraordinary income, access to secret opportunities, or luck reserved for the privileged few.

Nothing could be further from the truth.

The principles in this book are timeless, practical, and proven. They reflect the same foundations used by successful professionals, entrepreneurs, investors, and financially stable families across the world. What distinguishes those who achieve financial independence from those who don't is not intelligence or talent — it is knowledge, consistency, and the courage to act.

This work stands out because it bridges the gap between theory and real life. It speaks directly to the employee, the job seeker, the young adult, the entrepreneur, the parent, and the person rebuilding from difficult seasons. It provides clear direction for those who feel lost, practical steps for those seeking change, and deep insight for those ready to break generational patterns.

The chapters within guide the reader through mindset, skill-building, employment strategies, personal finance, investing, debt management, entrepreneurship, long-term planning, and legacy creation. Each concept is delivered in a conversational, relatable, and motivational style — making complex financial tools accessible to anyone willing to learn.

This book does more than teach financial principles.

It challenges the reader to expand their identity, to confront limiting beliefs, and to step boldly into a future shaped by intentional choices.

It is a manual for transformation — personal, financial, and generational. If you apply what you read here, consistently and courageously, your life will not remain the same.

Your journey to financial independence begins now. Turn the page.

◈ Chapter 1 — The Beginning

"Your financial journey doesn't start with money. It starts with a decision."

There comes a moment in every person's life when silence becomes loud. When you look at your finances — or the lack of them — and something in you whispers, "There has to be more than this."

This chapter is about that whisper.

It is about the moment you decide you are done surviving, done guessing, done stumbling, done living at the mercy of circumstances. It is the moment you say, "Enough."

Because financial independence does not begin with wealth. It begins with awareness, then decision, then alignment.

And today, you are stepping into that alignment.

—-

◈ The Power of a Decision

Most people think the first step to building wealth is earning more.

It isn't.

Some think it's saving.

It isn't.

Others think it's investing.

Not yet.

The first step — the root of every financial breakthrough — is deciding you deserve better.You cannot build a new life with an undecided mind.

Indecision keeps people trapped for decades — working jobs they hate, spending money they don't have, and hoping life will change "one day."

But "one day" is not a date on the calendar.

It's a choice.

The greatest transformation begins the moment you decide:
"I am ready to learn."
"I am ready to grow."
"I am ready to become disciplined."
"I am ready to take responsibility for my future."

This is where the journey begins.

—-

◈ The Mirror Moment

Every person who rises financially experiences what I call "the mirror moment."

It's when you sit down — maybe with a notebook, maybe with a quiet mind — and face your truth without excuses.

Not with shame.
Not with judgment.
With honesty.
You ask yourself:

✓ Where am I today financially?
✓ How did I get here?
✓ What habits are hurting me?
✓ What habits are helping me?
✓ What do I really want my life to look like?
✓ What am I willing to do differently?

This honesty is not comfortable, but it is liberating. The truth doesn't break you — it frees you.

Because once you know where you are, you can finally decide where you're going.

—-

Your "Why" — The Fuel of Change

Money on its own is not motivation.

If money motivated people, everyone would be financially independent.

Your why is deeper.

Your why is emotional.

Your why is personal.

<u>Examples:</u>

★ "I want to stop living paycheck to paycheck."

★ "I want to stop borrowing and feeling embarrassed."

★ "I want to give my children a better life."

★ "I want choices, not desperation."

★ "I want to retire with dignity."

★ "I don't want to depend on anyone."

★ "I want peace."

★ "I want freedom."

Your why becomes your anchor on the days you feel tired, distracted, or discouraged. Because there will be days when the old habits try to pull you back. But your why keeps you moving forward.

- **Write it down.**
- **Say it out loud.**
- **Return to it often.**

This is your foundation.

—-

◈ Vision — Seeing Beyond Today

Once the decision is made, and the why is clear, the next step is vision.

Financial independence is not built by accident. It is intentional. It requires direction.

So ask yourself:

- **What does financial freedom look like for me?**
- **How do I want to live?**
- **What level of stability do I want?**
- **What things do I want to stop worrying about?**
- **What kind of lifestyle do I want to create?**
- **What habits do I want to master?**
- **What kind of person do I want to become?"**

Your vision must be bigger than your current struggles. It must pull you forward with a quiet force.

Because vision gives you clarity. And clarity makes you unstoppable.

—-

◈ You Are Not Behind — You Are Beginning

Some people feel they started too late. Some feel they are too far behind. Some think their mistakes disqualify them.

But hear this clearly:

You are exactly on time for your own journey. Whether you're 18 or 45 or 60, the moment you decide to rise is the moment your life begins to shift.

No one is disqualified.

No one is too late.

No one is too far gone.

Your past brought you here. Your future begins now.

—-

◈ The Commitment to Change

Decision is powerful, but commitment is what transforms.

Commitment means:

showing up even when motivation fades, choosing discipline over feelings, learning skills even when they feel challenging, saving even when spending seems easier, investing even when you're scared, believing in yourself even when life tests you

When you commit, your financial life stops being an accident and starts becoming a masterpiece.

—-

◈ A Moment With You

Before we end this chapter, I want you to pause.

Take a breath.

Place your hand on your chest if you want.

And repeat this quietly to yourself:

"I choose to build a better future.

I choose financial independence.

And today, I begin."

There is power in this moment.

And this chapter marks the start of a story you will one day be proud you wrote.

◈ Chapter 2 — Mindset

"Wealth grows first in the mind, then in the bank."

Before money ever shows up in your hands, it must first exist in your mind.

The truth is simple but powerful:

Your financial life is a reflection of your inner world — your beliefs, your habits, your fears, your expectations, and the silent agreements you've made with yourself about what is possible.

This chapter is about transforming that inner world so that the outer one can finally change.

—-

◈ The Invisible Roots of Wealth

Most people don't struggle because they lack opportunity. They struggle because they lack the mindset to recognize or act on opportunity.

You may have heard this:

> If you give a poor mindset a million dollars, it will shrink. But if you give a wealthy mindset a hundred dollars, it will grow.

This is not about intelligence. It is about belief systems.

A person who believes "I can learn anything" grows.

A person who believes "Money is hard to get" keeps losing it.

A person who believes "I'll never be rich" begins living in ways that fulfill that prophecy.

Your mindset silently decides your financial future long before your actions do.

But here is the good news:

Mindset can be changed.

And once it changes, everything else follows.

—-

⟐ The Hidden Beliefs That Hold People Back

Everyone carries silent beliefs shaped by childhood, environment, culture, or painful experiences. Some of these beliefs limit how far we rise.

Do any of these sound familiar?

- **"I'm just not good with money."**
- **"People like me don't become wealthy."**
- **"Money always disappears."**
- **"Rich people are greedy."**
- **"Having money is embarrassing."**
- **"I don't deserve more."**
- **"I'll lose everything if I try."**
- **"Wealth is for the lucky."**

These beliefs act like invisible chains.

They create ceilings you can't see but always feel.

Your job in this chapter is to break them.

—-

⟐ Rewriting Your Money Identity

You cannot attract what you believe you are unworthy of. To become financially independent, you must begin to see yourself differently — not as someone who struggles...not as someone who is always behind...but as someone who is becoming disciplined, capable, and worthy of overflow.

Let this sink in:

- **You are not who your past says you are.**

- **You are who you decide to become.**

<u>Here's a simple exercise:</u>

Write down: "The kind of financially independent person I am becoming is..."

Then complete the sentence:

- Disciplined
- Focused
- Wise
- A learner
- Strategic
- Consistent
- Courageous
- Prepared
- Generous
- Intentional

Keep this list where you can see it.

Read it until it becomes part of you.

Identity drives behavior. Behavior shapes destiny.

—-

Your Mind: The Most Valuable Asset You Own

You may not have money now. You may not have connections. You may not have degrees or certifications yet. But you do have one thing:

Your mind-And what you feed it determines what it produces.

Feed your mind with: books, skills, wisdom(read the book of proverbs), financial knowledge, strong role models, disciplines that shape you, stories of people who started with nothing

Your mind becomes soil. What you plant grows.

Every day you learn something new about money is a day you step closer to financial independence.

—-

◈ The Difference Between a Scarcity Mindset & an Abundance Mindset

A scarcity mindset says:

- **"There's never enough."**
- **"I must hold onto everything."**
- **"If others succeed, I lose."**
- **"Opportunities are rare."**

An abundance mindset says:

- **"There's enough for me too."**
- **"Money flows when I use it wisely."**
- **"Opportunities increase when I prepare."**
- **"I can learn anything I need."**

Scarcity leads to fear. Abundance leads to action.

Scarcity shrinks your world. Abundance expands it.

Your mindset determines whether you survive financially... or rise beyond anything you once imagined.

—-

◈ The Courage to Believe in More

One of the bravest things you will ever do is believe that more is possible for you — even when your current life doesn't show it yet.

Wealth is not built by the comfortable. It is built by the courageous. By people willing to believe:

1. **In their potential**
2. **In their ability to learn**
3. **In their ability to rise**
4. **In their future**
5. **In their vision**

Even when no one else believes in them.

Let this chapter become your turning point. Not just in financial learning — but in identity, belief, and expectation.

—-

◈ A Moment With You

Pause.
Close your eyes if you want.
And say this softly:
"My mind is fertile ground.
My beliefs are shifting.
My future is expanding.
Wealth begins in me."
You are becoming the kind of person wealth feels safe to stay with.
When the mind rises, the life rises.

⟐ Chapter 3 — Starting From Zero

"Starting small is not a weakness; it is a strategy."

There is a myth that stops millions of people from moving forward financially: the belief that you need a "big start" to change your life.

A big salary.

A big business.

A big investment.

A big opportunity.

A big blessing.

But the truth — the real truth — is this:

Most successful people began with nothing but hunger, humility, and a willingness to start small.

Starting from zero is not a disadvantage.

It is clarity.

It is focus.

It is fuel.

This chapter is your permission to begin exactly where you are, without shame, fear, or comparison.

—-

⟐ Why Starting Small Works

Starting small forces you to do the one thing wealth requires: **Learn.**

When you start small:

- You learn to manage money before handling bigger amounts.
- You develop discipline that wealth requires.
- You become creative with limited resources.
- You cultivate gratitude for small progress.

- You grow consistently instead of recklessly.

Large success built on weak foundations collapses. But small beginnings build unshakable foundations.

Starting small is not a delay to your wealth — it is the training ground that prepares you for it.

—-

◈ <u>The Power of Micro Progress</u>

You do not need giant steps. You need consistent ones.

Examples:

- Saving just $1 a day becomes $30 a month.
- Earning an extra $40 a week becomes $160 a month.
- Reducing one unnecessary expense can save hundreds a year.
- Learning one new skill can double your income later.
- Paying an extra $10 monthly toward debt can shorten years.

The progress seems small — until you look back one year later and realize your entire life shifted.

Small progress compounds into big results.

—-

◈ <u>If You Are Unemployed or Starting Over</u>

When you have no job, little income, or you feel like you're at the bottom, the world may look heavy — but this is often where the greatest transformations begin.

<u>Here is your starting strategy:</u>

1. Reduce your financial pressure
Before earning more, reduce what drains you.
Look at:

- The unnecessary subscriptions
- Impulse spending
- Expensive habits
- Avoidable transport costs
- Lifestyle choices that don't align with your goals

You cannot rise while carrying unnecessary weight.
2. Identify what skills you already have
Everyone has something they can monetize.
Ask yourself:

- What do people often ask me for help with?
- What comes naturally to me?
- What problems can I solve for others?
- What small service could I offer in my community?

You don't need a degree to start earning. You need a problem to solve.
3. Start with low-cost, low-risk income streams
These could be simple things like:

- offering freelance services
- selling items online
- assisting businesses with small tasks
- tutoring
- helping with errands
- home-based services
- social media content services

A trickle becomes a stream. A stream becomes a river.

4. Learn aggressively

- Watch free tutorials.
- Read financial books.
- Take basic courses.
- Learn online skills.

Learning turns your zero into something powerful.

—-

◈ If You Are Employed and Want More

Starting small doesn't mean staying small.
Here's how you grow when you already have a job:
1. Become excellent at your current role
Your paycheck is tied to your value.
Increase your skill — increase your income.
2. Learn one high-value skill outside work
This could be:

- Project management
- Coding
- Design
- Data analysis
- Digital marketing
- Communication skills
- Public speaking
- Leadership

One upgraded skill can elevate your entire life.
3. Start a micro-side hustle
Not a giant business that drains you —
a simple one that earns while you learn.

4. Save and invest early

Even small amounts invested consistently become wealth over time.

—-

◈Transforming "Small" Into "Momentum"

The difference between people who rise and people who stay stuck is not talent. It is momentum.

Momentum begins with one small action, such as: saving your first $10, learning one new skill today, sending one job application, watching one learning video, joining one financial group, reading one chapter of a book, planning one small business idea

These tiny actions open doors you cannot see yet.

—-

◈ Comparison — The Enemy of Progress

One of the biggest killers of financial growth is comparison.

You see someone your age with a car, a house, a high-paying job, a successful business — and suddenly your progress feels small.

But hear this:

Someone else's timeline is not your deadline.

Comparison blinds you to your own growth. It makes you forget that every successful person once started at zero.

Your journey is uniquely yours. Your progress is real. Your story is unfolding exactly as it needs to.

Stay focused on your lane. Stay rooted in your pace.

—-

◈ A Moment With You

Close your eyes for a moment.
Take a deep breath.
And tell yourself:
"I honor my small beginnings.
I build with what I have.
I rise from where I stand.
Starting small is my power."

Your zero is not a void — it is the soil where your new life is being planted.

◊ Chapter 4 — Climbing the Corporate Ladder

"You rise in the workplace not by being seen, but by making yourself valuable."

Many people think career growth is about being liked, noticed, or loudly ambitious.

But true elevation — the kind that leads to promotions, influence, stability, and higher income — comes from one simple truth:

Value rises. Always.

You don't climb the corporate ladder because someone favors you. You climb because your work becomes essential, undeniable, and impossible to ignore.

This chapter is your roadmap to becoming that kind of person.

—-

◊ The Mindset Shift: From Employee to Asset

There is a difference between being hired and being needed.

Employees do tasks. Assets create impact.

Employees wait for instructions. Assets solve problems before being asked.

Employees think only of today's work.

Assets think of the company's future.

When you shift from "I work for them" to "I contribute value," everything changes: your confidence, your opportunities, your income, and the way leadership sees you.

Companies promote assets, not workers.

—-

◊ The Three Pillars of Career Elevation

1. Competence — Become the Best at Your Role

Master your job so fully that people trust you without hesitation.

To elevate:

- Understand your job deeper than your job description.
- Learn the skills others avoid.
- Be reliable, accurate, and consistent.
- Deliver work before the deadline.
- Learn the tools and technologies your team uses.
- Ask: "How can this be done better?"

Competence is not about perfection, it's about progress, precision, and ownership.

When you become excellent, people notice. When you become irreplaceable, they reward you.

2. Character — How You Carry Yourself

People often underestimate this, but character elevates careers faster than skill alone.

Strong character means:

- Showing integrity even when no one is watching
- Communicating clearly and respectfully
- Staying calm under pressure
- Taking responsibility for mistakes
- Being dependable, not dramatic

- Treating colleagues with respect
- Managing emotions, not spreading negativity

Character builds trust. Trust unlocks opportunities.

People may question your skills at times — but they should never question your character.

3. Contribution — Going Beyond the Minimum

Promotions don't come from doing what you're told. They come from doing what is needed.

Here's what high-value contributors do:

- Solve problems, not complain about them
- Think ahead instead of reacting
- Bring ideas to improve processes
- Support teammates during busy seasons
- Volunteer for projects that stretch them
- Make their manager's job easier
- See the big picture of the company
- Learn skills that fill gaps in the team

People who consistently add value, becomes the first ones to be considered for leadership roles.

Because leadership is not a position, it is behavior.

◈ The Skill Upgrade Strategy

In every industry, there are certain skills that accelerate promotions and income.

These are high-value skills such as:

- Leadership
- Communication
- Emotional intelligence
- Project management
- Data analysis
- Digital literacy
- Presentation skills
- Teamwork and collaboration
- Conflict resolution
- Customer service mastery

Every skill you add becomes a ladder you climb. Learning transforms you from replaceable to essential.

—-

◈ Visibility Without Noise

Many think they need to be loud to get noticed. But true visibility comes from consistency, not noise.

You become visible when:

- Your work is always high quality
- You deliver results without excuses
- You communicate with clarity
- You stay dependable under pressure
- You show initiative

People trust you with important tasks

You don't need to shout. Let your work speak loudly for you.

Silent consistency is stronger than loud chaos.

—-

◈ Conflict, Jealousy & Office Politics

No workplace is perfect. You will meet people who misunderstand you, compete with you, or feel threatened by your growth.

Remember this:

Your focus is on elevation, not distraction.

To overcome workplace negativity:

- Avoid gossip
- Stay professional
- Address issues calmly
- Don't take things personally
- Protect your reputation
- Let your results defend you

Not everyone will clap for you — and that's okay. You didn't come to be liked. You came to rise.

—-

◈ Asking for Promotion or Raises

Promotions don't always come automatically. Sometimes you must ask — but with strategy.

Here's how:

1. Document your achievements.

List the projects you've led, solved, or improved.

2. Understand the company's goals.

Show how your work contributes to them.

3. Be specific.

Explain why you're ready for the next step.

4. Show how you've grown.

Highlight new skills and responsibilities you've taken on.

5. Ask with confidence, not fear.

You're not begging — you're presenting evidence. If they say "not yet," don't break.

Ask what you need to develop, work on it, and return stronger.

Your career belongs to you — not to their hesitation.

—-

◈ A Moment With You

Take a breath.

Place your hand on your heart.

And say softly:

"I rise by becoming valuable.

I elevate by becoming excellent.

I grow by becoming intentional.

I am building a career that supports my future."

When you shift who you are, your workplace shifts how it treats you.

◈ Chapter 5 — Networking

"The doors you walk through often belong to the people you know."

Money is powerful.

Skills are powerful.

Discipline is powerful.

But relationships — the right relationships — can change your life faster than anything else.

People often misunderstand networking. They think it's about collecting contacts, shaking hands, or pretending to be friendly.

But real networking is something deeper, quieter, and far more meaningful. It is about connection, not performance. Value, not manipulation.

Long-term relationships, not quick favors.

The right relationship can shortcut your journey by years.

This chapter will show you how to build those relationships — no matter your personality, background, or starting point.

—-

◈ Why You Cannot Succeed Alone

One of the biggest traps people fall into is the "I can do it alone" mindset.

But here's the truth:

No one rises alone.

No one succeeds alone.

No one grows alone.

Every successful person — every entrepreneur, every leader, every professional — has benefited from:

- Guidance
- Connections

- Opportunities
- Recommendation
- Collaboration
- Mentorship
- Support
- Referrals

Someone somewhere opened a door for them.Your job is not to climb alone.

Your job is to connect wisely.

—-

<u>⟐ Networking Is Not Using People — It Is Aligning With People</u>

Healthy networking means:

- I support you
- You support me
- We grow together
- It is mutual.
- It is honest.
- It is respectful.

- It is built on shared values or shared goals.

<u>People misuse networking when they:</u>

✓ Only reach out when they want something
✓ Pretend to care but only want access
✓ Fake interest for personal benefit
✓ Drain others without offering value

This is why many people fear networking — they think it's fake. But networking rooted in authenticity is not fake. It is human. And humans rise together.

—-

◈How to Build Genuine Connections

1. Lead With Value

Before asking for anything, give something.

Your value could be:

- Sharing information
- Offering help
- Recommending a tool or resource
- Introducing someone to someone else
- Appreciating someone's work
- Supporting their projects
- Asking thoughtful questions

When people feel valued, they open doors naturally.

—-

2. Be Interested, Not Interesting

Most people approach networking by trying to impress. But the strongest connections form when you:

- **Listen deeply**
- **Ask genuine questions**
- **Show curiosity**
- **Show respect**
- **Remember their experiences**

- **Understand their journey**

People connect with people who care — not people who perform.

—-

3. Stay Connected Without Being Desperate

You don't need to message every day. You don't need to force conversations.

You simply need to:

a. Check in occasionally
b. Congratulate them on achievements
c. Share something meaningful to them
d. Reply thoughtfully when they reach out
e. Show consistency without pressure

This keeps the bridge open.

—-

4. Be the Person People Want to Recommend

<u>People only recommend you if:</u>

You are reliable

You deliver quality

You communicate well

You act with integrity

You respect their reputation

You follow through

When you become trustworthy, doors open without you knocking.

—-

◈Digital Networking — Your New Superpower

You don't need to be outgoing. You don't need to attend events if you don't enjoy them.

Today, networking is global and digital. You can build powerful relationships through:

- LinkedIn
- Facebook groups
- WhatsApp communities
- Twitter/X
- Instagram
- Online courses
- Business forums
- Mentorship platforms

A single message could connect you with someone who changes your life forever.

—-

◈ Building a Network When You Feel You Have Nothing

Many people hesitate to network because they feel:

- Unqualified
- Inexperienced
- Shy
- Behind
- Insecure
- Unworthy
- Afraid of rejection

But hear this: You have value — even if you don't see it yet.

<u>You can offer:</u>

Your time

Your willingness to learn

Your respect

Your consistency

Your gratitude

Your enthusiasm

Your loyalty

Your ideas

Your skills, even if small. People appreciate sincerity more than perfection.

—-

<u>⟐ The Power of Community</u>

Do not walk alone. Join communities that lift you.

<u>Communities for:</u>

Financial literacy

Career growth

Entrepreneurship

Investing

Skill-building

Personal development

Networking

Accountability

<u>A strong community gives you:</u>

Encouragement

Direction

Answers
Motivation
Opportunity
Collaboration
Support
Clarity

And sometimes, it gives you the one connection that changes everything.

—-

◈ A Moment With You

Place your hand over your heart.
Take a breath.
And say softly:
"I build connections that lift me higher.
I attract the right people into my life.
I give value and receive value.
The doors meant for me will open."

Your network is a bridge — and every bridge takes you closer to a future bigger than the one you're living now.

◈ Chapter 6 — Spending Wisely

"Control your spending, or your spending will control your life."

Money is not only about what you earn — it is equally about what you keep. Some people earn well but remain broke. Others earn little yet manage to build savings, investments, and stability.

The difference is not income. It is self-control, clarity, and intentional spending.

This chapter is about learning how to take command of your money — so your money no longer commands you.

—-

◈ The Truth About Spending

Most people don't realize how easily money slips away. Not through big expenses, but through tiny, unplanned decisions: ,a snack here, a subscription there, a ride you didn't need, impulse purchases, emotional spending, unnecessary upgrades, unplanned social outings

Money doesn't disappear — it leaks.

And those leaks quietly drown your financial progress. Before you earn more, you must fix the leaks.

—-

◈Needs vs Wants — The Quiet Battle

If you want financial independence, you must master the difference between need and want.

A need supports your life, responsibilities, or survival. A want supports your feelings.

There is nothing wrong with wanting things. But you must know when you can afford them.

Here's a simple rule:

Needs build your foundation. Wants should reward your discipline — not replace it.

When your wants become bigger than your discipline, your money becomes your enemy.

—-

◈ Emotional Spending — The Hidden Trap

We live in a world where spending is emotional. People buy because they feel: ,stressed, lonely, bored, insecure, pressured, sad, or excited.

This is why some people save nothing — not because they lack income, but because buying gives temporary relief.

But your emotions cannot manage your money. Your money requires logic, purpose, and planning.

Ask yourself whenever you are tempted to buy something:

"Do I want this, or is something in me wanting comfort?"

This single question will save you from countless regrets.

—-

◈The Power of Delayed Gratification

Successful people delay gratification, not enjoyment.

They trade:

- Instant pleasure for long-term peace
- Short-term excitement for long-term comfort
- Temporary happiness for lasting stability
- Impulse for intention

Here is a simple rule to transform your life:

If you can delay it, you don't need it.

Buying something tomorrow instead of today changes nothing. But the discipline it builds changes everything.

—-

⟐ The 48-Hour Rule

Before making ANY non-essential purchase: Wait 48 hours. If after 48 hours: you still need it. Then it still makes sense, because It aligns with your budget, it does not set you back

...then buy it with confidence.

Impulse fades with time. Clarity grows with patience.

—-

⟐ The Lifestyle Trap

Many people destroy their finances trying to LOOK financially successful instead of actually becoming successful. This is called lifestyle inflation.

It happens when:

You get a raise → you increase expenses

You get a better job → you upgrade lifestyle

You start earning more → you spend more

You feel pressured → you show off

The reality?

Lifestyle inflation keeps you broke at a higher level.

Here is your protection:

As your income rises, keep your lifestyle stable — and let your savings rise instead.

Wealth grows in silence, not in display.

—-

◈ Practical Tools to Spend Wisely

1. The Weekly Money Check-in

Every week, sit down for 5 minutes and review:

What you spent

What you wasted

What you can improve

Awareness is power.

—-

2. Use Cash for "Danger Zones"

If you overspend on food, entertainment, or transport, withdraw a fixed cash amount weekly. When the cash finishes, you stop spending. Simple. Effective.

—-

3. Make a "Don't Buy List"

These are things you must avoid until your finances stabilize:

Debt-funded luxuries

Frequent takeout

Impulsive clothing

Unnecessary subscriptions

Emotional spending triggers

Your financial future begins with what you refuse.

—-

4. The Three-Quote Rule for Big Purchases
Before buying anything expensive:

1. Get three prices

1. Compare quality

1. Check reviews

1. Wait 48 hours

You'd be shocked how many "must haves" were never necessary.

—-

◈ The Strength to Say No
Saying "no" to others is hard.
Saying "no" to yourself is harder.
But if you cannot say "no" to your desires, your dreams will say "no" to you.
Every time you say:
"No, I'll wait."
"No, I don't need that right now."
"No, that doesn't align with my goals."

...you gain power.

You build discipline.
You take control.
Your future thanks you.

—-

◈ A Moment With You

Pause for a moment.
Take a deep breath.
Then whisper:
"I control my money.
I control my desires.
I choose my future over temporary feelings."
Wise spending is not deprivation.
It is direction. And it is one of the most powerful tools you'll ever master.

◈ Chapter 7 — Saving With Purpose

"Saving is not a sacrifice. It is self-respect for your future."

For many people, the word saving feels heavy — like punishment, restriction, or deprivation.

But saving is not about denying yourself. It is about honoring the version of you that will exist tomorrow, next year, and ten years from now.

- You don't save because you're scared.
- You save because you are wise.
- You save because your future matters.
- You save because your dreams deserve funding.
- You save because financial peace is better than financial performance.

This chapter will teach you how to save in a way that feels empowering, meaningful, and purposeful — not miserable or limiting.

—-

◈ Why Saving Matters More Than You Think

Saving is the foundation of financial independence because:

- **Opportunities require money**
- **Emergencies require money**
- **Investments require money**
- **Peace of mind requires money**
- **Stability requires money**
- **Freedom requires money**

When you save, you create options.

When you don't save, life chooses for you.

Savings are not about the amount — they are about the habit.

Even 100 shillings or 1 dollar consistently saved is more powerful than 10,000 saved once.

Small seeds still grow trees.

—-

◈ Savings = Self-Protection

Life is unpredictable.

People lose jobs.

Businesses struggle.

Expenses appear suddenly.

Illnesses come without warning.

Family members need help.

If you have no savings, every crisis feels like drowning.

But when you save, storms still come — you just stay afloat.

Saving gives you stability in a world that offers none.

—-

◈Purposeful Saving vs Random Saving

Most people save randomly: when they feel like it, when money is left over, when life is calm, when nothing urgent is happening

This is why their savings don't grow — because emotions can never grow money.

Purposeful savings are different, Purposeful savings are intentional, structured, and aligned with your goals.

Ask yourself:

"Why am I saving?"

The why strengthens your discipline.

Your why might be: to build an emergency fund, to invest, to start a business, to buy land or a home, to pay school fees, to travel, to give your children a better life, to retire peacefully, to escape financial anxiety.

Whatever your why is — hold it close.

It will push you when motivation fades.

—-

◈The 5 Golden Rules of Saving With Purpose

1. Save First, Spend After

Most people do the opposite:

They spend, then try to save what's left. But there is never anything left.

The wealthy apply a simple rule:

Pay yourself first. Before you pay bills, before you buy anything, before you send money anywhere — you save a portion of your income. Even if it is small. Especially if it is small.

Small beginnings become strong habits.

—-

2. Automate Your Savings

Relying on willpower is unreliable.

Automate:

- A standing order
- An automatic transfer
- A mobile money auto-deposit
- A SACCO auto-deduction

When saving becomes automatic, you don't have to choose — it just happens.

Make saving a system, not a struggle.

—-

3. Have Separate Saving Accounts

Mixing your savings with your daily spending is the fastest way to sabotage yourself.

<u>Have specific accounts for:</u>

- Emergency savings
- Long-term goals
- Investment funds
- SACCO contributions
- Short-term projects

When money has a home, it doesn't get lost.

—-

4. Save a Percentage, Not an Amount

Your income will always change. Set a percentage so your savings grow with you.

<u>Recommended:</u>

- 10% minimum
- 20–30% ideal
- 50% during seasons of high income

Percentage-based saving makes your growth automatic.

—-

5. Increase Your Saving Rate as You Earn More

As your income grows:

1. **Don't upgrade your lifestyle immediately**
1. **Don't increase unnecessary expenses**
1. **Don't fall into the "I deserve it" trap**

Instead:

Increase your savings rate first, then your lifestyle later.
This strategy builds wealth faster than anything else.

—-

◈ Saving Without Feeling Miserable

You don't have to suffer to save.
You don't need to live like a monk.
You don't have to deny yourself joy.

Here's how to save joyfully:

★ Budget some money for enjoyment
★ Use discounts, sales, and offers
★ Avoid impulsive spending
★ Simplify your lifestyle, don't suffocate it
★ Find free or low-cost entertainment
★ Celebrate milestones
★ Track your progress

★ Surround yourself with people who respect your goals

Saving feels miserable only when you compare yourself to others. When you focus on your path, saving feels empowering.

—-

◈The Power of SACCOs & Collective Saving

SACCOs (or cooperatives) are one of the most powerful tools for building savings and credit discipline.

They help you:

★ Save consistently
★ Avoid spending temptations
★ Build creditworthiness
★ Access affordable loans
★ Benefit from dividends
★ Stay accountable
★ Grow long-term wealth

Joining a SACCO is like joining a community of disciplined dreamers.

You rise together.

—-

◈ A Vision for the Future

Think of the future version of you: peaceful, stable, protected, confident and free

That version is built by today's discipline.

Every coin you save whispers:

"I am building something."

"I am preparing for greatness."
"My future matters."
You are not sacrificing today — you are investing in tomorrow.

—-

◈ A Moment With You

Close your eyes.
Breathe slowly.
And say:
"I honor my future self.
I save with purpose.
Every amount I save strengthens me.
I am building a life of stability, peace, and freedom."
Your savings are a silent promise. A promise you are keeping every day.

◈ Chapter 8 — Investing

"Every investment is a seed — plant consistently and the harvest becomes inevitable."

Saving protects you. But investing grows you. Saving gives you stability. But investing gives you freedom.

You cannot become financially independent by saving alone. Savings keep your money safe — but investments make your money multiply.

This chapter will guide you through the world of investing in a simple, practical, and empowering way — so you can plant seeds today that will feed you for the rest of your life.

—-

◈ Why Investing Is Non-Negotiable

If you keep your money only in a savings account:

- **Inflation eats it**
- **Life becomes more expensive**
- **Your money remains the same while your needs grow**
- **Opportunities pass you by**

But when you invest, your money starts working for you — even when you sleep.

Think of it this way:

****Your salary pays your bills. Your investments pay your future.****

Every financially free person you admire became free because of one thing:

They invested.

—-

◈ The Mindset of an Investor

Before learning where to invest, you must understand how investors think.

Investors:

- ★ Think long-term
- ★ Understand risks
- ★ Diversify
- ★ Do research
- ★ Stay patient
- ★ Avoid emotional decisions
- ★ Accept that growth is gradual
- ★ Stay consistent

Investing is not gambling.

It is not a get-rich-quick scheme.

It is not for people seeking overnight results.

Investing is for people who are ready to plant seeds and let time work its miracle.

—-

◈ The Golden Rule of Investing: Start Small

You don't need thousands.

You don't need perfect knowledge.

You don't need to wait for "the right moment."

The perfect time to invest does not exist. But the right time does:

Right now.

Start with what you have:

$1

$5

$10
KES 100
KES 500
KES 1,000

The amount does not matter. Your consistency does.
Small investments grow into large portfolios.

—-

◈ Types of Investments You Can Start With

1. Stocks (Shares)

You buy a small piece of a company.
If the company grows, your money grows.
Benefits:

- High long-term returns
- Easy to start
- Affordable
- Passive income through dividends

Risk:

1. Prices may fluctuate
2. Requires patience

Stocks are seeds — slow growing but powerful.

—-

2. Government Bonds & Treasury Bills

You lend money to the government and earn interest.
Benefits:
Safe
Predictable
Good for beginners
Long-term stability

Risk:
Lower returns than stocks, but safer

These are like planting trees — steady, reliable, protective.

—-

3. Mutual Funds / Unit Trusts
Professionals invest your money for you.
Benefits:
Easy for beginners
Low risk
You can start with very little
Diversified portfolio

Think of it as group farming — everyone contributes, everyone benefits.

—-

4. Real Estate (Land, Property, Rentals)
One of the strongest long-term investments.
Benefits:

★ Value usually increases
★ Can generate rental income
★ Tangible asset

<u>**Risk:**</u>

Requires patience and research
Higher starting cost

Property is the mountain of investments — slow to build, impossible to shake.

—-

5. SACCO Shares & Dividends

When you join a SACCO, you can buy shares and earn dividends yearly.

<u>**Benefits:**</u>

Steady annual returns
Low entry cost
Safe and regulated

SACCO shares are excellent for disciplined, long-term growth.

—-

6. Business Investments

<u>You can invest in:</u>

1. Your own business
2. Partnerships

3. Side hustles
4. Income-generating projects

High risk, but often high reward. This is where many millionaires come from.

—-

⟐ The Rule of Multiplying Money

Investing has something magical called compound interest.

This is when:

Your money earns money, then that money earns more money and the cycle continues. It's growth on top of growth. Earnings on top of earnings.

It is slow at first — then suddenly powerful.

Albert Einstein called compound interest the "eighth wonder of the world."

You don't need force to grow money. You need time and consistency.

—-

⟐ How to Know an Investment Is Safe

Before investing anywhere, ask yourself:

1. Do I understand it?

If you don't understand, don't invest.

2. Is it regulated by the government?

3. Is the company or platform reliable?

4. Are there clear, transparent terms?

5. Do returns sound realistic?

(If they sound too good to be true — they are.)

6. Is there a history of payouts?

7. Am I using money I can afford to lock away?

Never invest out of pressure, excitement, or fear of missing out. Invest out of clarity.

—-

◈ The Patient Investor Always Wins

Investing is a long-term game. You don't harvest the day you plant. You don't become wealthy after one month. You don't see big results instantly. But over time, your investments form a financial forest around you.

People who lose money are those who:

1. panic
2. rush
3. try to get rich fast
4. compare themselves
5. quit too soon

Patience is your greatest investment skill.

—-

◈ A Vision of Your Future

Imagine 2 years from now:

Your stocks have grown, your SACCO dividends arrive, your emergency fund is solid, your money grows without your effort, you sleep peacefully because your financial foundation is strong, opportunities become affordable, you no longer fear the future

This is what investing gives you —

quiet confidence.

—-

◈ A Moment With You

Put your hand on your heart.
Breathe.
Say softly:
"Every seed I plant will grow.
My money multiplies.
I invest with wisdom, patience, and purpose.
My future is abundant."
Your wealth will not happen in one day —
but it will happen because of what you do every day.

◈ Chapter 9 — Escaping Debt

"Debt is a silent thief of your dreams. Guard them fiercely."

Debt does not shout.

It whispers.

It creeps quietly into your life — one loan here, one purchase there — until one day you wake up and realize:

Your future has been mortgaged.

Debt steals: your peace, your income, your options,your confidence, your dreams, your sleep, your progress

And because debt feels normal in society, many people don't realize how damaging it is until they can no longer breathe financially.

This chapter is about reclaiming your freedom — and learning how to escape the silent trap that keeps millions stuck.

—-

◈ Understanding Debt: Friend or Enemy?

Not all debt is evil.

Some debts are strategic.

Some debts help you build.

But most debts?

They drain you.

There are two categories:

1. Good Debt

Debt used to build assets or increase your earning power.

Examples:

1. Loans for education that increases income
2. Business loans (if managed well)

3. Mortgages for property that appreciates
4. Investment loans with clear, safe returns

2. Bad Debt

Debt used to buy things that lose value or disappear fast.

Examples:

1. Impulse purchases
2. Lifestyle upgrades
3. Unnecessary luxury items
4. Borrowing for clothes, food, entertainment
5. Payday loans
6. Mobile app loans
7. "Buy now, pay later" temptations

Good debt builds you. Bad debt buries you.

Most people are drowning because they confuse the two.

—-

◈ The Psychology of Debt

Debt is not just financial — it is emotional.

People borrow because of: pressure, impatience,embarrassment, comparison, insecurity, emergencies, wanting instant results

Debt solves the moment but steals the years. Understanding why you borrow is the first step to breaking free.

Ask yourself honestly:

"Do I borrow because I need to, or because I lack discipline?"

This question alone can transform your entire financial journey.

—-

♦ The Real Cost of Debt

Debt is not just the amount you owe.
It is:

> The interest, the fees, the penalties, the stress, the delay in your goals, the lost opportunities, the lost investments, the pressure, the mental exhaustion

If you owe $500, you don't owe $500.
You owe all the dreams that $500 could have built.
Debt takes you backwards while life keeps moving forward.

—-

♦ How to Escape Debt — Step by Step

1. Stop Borrowing Immediately

You cannot escape a hole while digging deeper.
Pause.
Freeze all unnecessary borrowing.
Say "no" even when it feels hard.
Freedom begins with refusing to go deeper.

—-

2. List Every Debt You Owe

Write them down clearly:

Lender
Total amount
Interest rate
Due dates
Penalties
Priority level

Seeing your debts on paper gives you control. Fear hides in the unknown.

—-

3. Use the Avalanche Method (Fastest)

Pay off the highest-interest debt first.

This method reduces the amount of money you lose to interest and helps you escape debt faster.

—-

4. Use the Snowball Method (Most Motivating)

If you need motivation, pay off the smallest debt first. Each victory gives you energy to keep going. Momentum builds confidence.

—-

5. Cut Unnecessary Expenses Temporarily

Your savings must now become your weapon.

Reduce:

- Eating out
- Subscriptions
- Impulse spending
- Luxuries
- Social habits
- Wasteful routines

This is temporary — but freedom is permanent.

—-

6. Increase Your Income

You cannot escape big debt with small income.
Consider:

- **side hustles**
- **overtime**
- **freelancing**
- **selling unused items**
- **skills-based services**
- **part-time gigs**

This extra money should go straight into debt repayment, not lifestyle upgrades.

—-

7. Negotiate With Lenders

Many people don't know this, but lenders often agree to:
Reduced penalties
Extended dates
Restructured payments
Lowered interest
Settlement discounts

All you need to do is ask confidently and calmly. You are not begging — you are negotiating your freedom.

—-

8. Create a Debt-Free Plan

Put everything into a structured plan:

- How much to pay weekly or monthly

- Which debts to target first
- Your debt-free target date
- Your income sources
- Your reduced expenses

A plan gives you direction. Direction gives you hope.

—-

◈ Protecting Yourself From Future Debt

1. Build an Emergency Fund

This stops you from borrowing during crisis.

2. Create sinking funds

Money set aside for predictable expenses like school fees, rent, holidays.

3. Live below your means

Not forever — just until you stabilize.

4. Avoid borrowing for lifestyle

You cannot impress people who don't even fund your life.

5. Delay gratification

Patience builds wealth.

Impatience builds debt.

—-

◈ The Freedom On the Other Side

When you escape debt, something beautiful happens: your mind becomes calm, your income becomes yours again, your goals feel possible, saving becomes easier, investing becomes natural, peace returns, opportunities open, confidence rises

Debt is a prison. Freedom is possible.

And you are already doing the work to break out.

—-

◈ A Moment With You

Close your eyes.

Breathe deeply.

Say:

"Debt does not define me.

My future is bigger than my past.

Every step I take leads to freedom.

I am breaking every financial chain."

You are not just escaping debt — you are reclaiming your life.

—-

◈ Chapter 10 — Emergency Preparedness

"Peace comes from knowing you're ready for what life brings."

Life is beautiful — but unpredictable. No matter how disciplined, organized, or prepared you are, unexpected events will still arise:

a. sudden illness

a. job loss

a. family emergencies

a. car or home repairs

a. economic shifts

a. natural disasters

a. urgent travel

a. business slowdowns

These moments are not always avoidable... but financial suffering during them is avoidable — when you prepare.

Emergency preparedness is not fear-based.

It is wisdom-based.

It is not pessimism.

It is positioning.

It is not worrying.

It is being ready.

This chapter teaches you how to create emotional calm and financial security for moments that would break others.

—-

◈ Why You Need an Emergency Plan

Most people don't fail financially because they are irresponsible —they fail because they are unprepared.

One unexpected event can:

- wipe out your savings
- push you into debt
- delay your goals
- destroy your progress
- increase your stress
- reduce your confidence

But when you're prepared, emergencies feel manageable. You become steady. You respond with clarity, not panic.

Emergency planning gives you the confidence to live life without fear of the unknown.

—-

◈ The Emergency Fund — Your Safety Net

An emergency fund is money set aside only for true emergencies.

It is not for: outings,holidays, clothes, entertainment, or impulse decisions It is for moments that threaten your stability.

The recommended amount is:
3 to 6 months of living expenses.
If your monthly expenses are $300, aim for:
$900 minimum
$1800 ideal

If your monthly expenses are KES 30,000, aim for:
KES 90,000 minimum
KES 180,000 ideal

If this feels impossible, start where you are.
Even KES 500 or $5 a week is progress.

—-

◈ Where to Keep Your Emergency Fund

Your emergency fund should be: separate from your main account, easy to access but not too easy, safe, stable, and protected

Good options include:

- A SACCO savings account
- A money market fund
- A high-yield savings account
- A dedicated bank account with no ATM card

Do not keep your emergency fund in:

Your M-Pesa main balance

Your daily-use bank account

Risky investments

Cash at home (unsafe and tempting to touch)

The goal is: easy to withdraw when needed, but difficult to misuse.

—-

⟐ Understanding What Counts as a Real Emergency

To protect your emergency fund, you must define what qualifies.

A real emergency is: health crisis, job loss, urgent family situations, unavoidable repairs, legal/medical emergencies, sudden income interruption, natural disaster, essential relocation

NOT an emergency: a birthday party, new clothes, impulse travel, a night out, upgrading electronics, entertaining pressure from friends, "I just felt like it."

Your emergency fund is for survival, not comfort.

—-

⟐ How to Build an Emergency Fund Step by Step

1. Calculate Your Monthly Expenses

List essential expenses:

Rent

Food

Transport

Utilities
Medical costs
School fees
Debt payments

Multiply the total by 3–6.

Now you know your target.

—-

2. Start Small but Start Now

Even if all you can save is:
$1 a day
$5 a week
KES 100 daily
KES 500 weekly

That's enough. Consistency beats amount.

—-

3. Automate the Deposits

Set a standing order or scheduled transfer. When saving becomes automatic, your future becomes safer.

—-

4. Use Windfalls Wisely

Whenever you receive: bonuses, tax refunds, gifted money, extra income, business profit, Put a portion into your emergency fund.

Future-you will thank you.

—-

5. Protect the Fund — Don't Touch It

This is the hardest part. Only touch your emergency fund in true emergencies.

Every time you avoid using it unnecessarily, your future becomes stronger.

—-

◈ Create a Crisis Plan

Emergency preparedness isn't just about money. It's also about clarity.

Write down:

Who you call first in a crisis
Alternative income ideas
Health insurance details
SACCO contacts
Important documents
People who can help
Monthly survival expenses
Quick ways to earn money if needed

In a crisis, panic makes your mind cloudy.

A written plan brings calm and direction.

—-

◈ The Power of Insurance

Insurance is protection — not an expense.

Consider having:

- ★ Medical insurance
- ★ Life insurance (if you have dependents)
- ★ Vehicle insurance
- ★ Home or rental insurance
- ★ Business insurance

Insurance is cheaper than the disasters it protects you from.

—-

◈ Preparing Emotionally for Emergencies

Emergencies test more than your wallet.
They test your:
Faith
Resilience
Discipline
Decisions
Patience
Courage

When you prepare financially, your emotions stay steady.You respond with wisdom, not fear. You stand strong, not shaken.

This calmness is priceless.

—-

◈ The Peace You Gain

- Imagine having:
- Money ready for any crisis
- No fear of unexpected events
- Confidence in your stability
- The ability to protect your family
- A sense of control over your life
- Peace that cannot be shaken

This is the gift of preparation.

Peace is not luck. Peace is planning.

—-

◈ **A Moment With You**

Place your hand on your heart.
Take a slow breath.
Say softly:
"I am prepared.
I am protected.
I am steady.
I plan for tomorrow with wisdom.
Peace lives in my preparation."

Emergencies no longer have the power to break you — because you are building strength in advance.

◈ Chapter 11 — Budgeting

"A budget is not a cage. It is a compass."

For many people, the word budget sounds restrictive — like a set of rules meant to suffocate joy and limit enjoyment. But that is the wrong picture.

A budget is not a prison.

A budget is freedom with direction.

A budget is clarity.

A budget is ownership of your life.

A budget is the map that guides your money toward your dreams instead of letting it wander blindly.

This chapter will show you how to create a budget that is simple, realistic, empowering, and easy to maintain — no suffering, no overwhelm, no confusion.

—-

◈ The Real Purpose of Budgeting

A budget isn't about saying:

"I can't."

"I'm restricted."

"I'm suffering."

"I'm limited."

A budget is about saying:

"I choose where my money goes."

"I am in control."

"My goals matter."

"My future matters."

Your budget is your plan.

Without a plan, money disappears.

With a plan, money obeys.

Budgeting is simply this:

Telling your money where to go instead of wondering where it went.

—-

⟐ Why Most People Fail at Budgeting

People fail at budgeting because they: create unrealistic plans, try to copy someone else's system, forget to include fun, ignore their real habits, try too hard to be perfect, use complex spreadsheets, rely on willpower instead of structure, feel guilty when they slip, focus only on restricting don't review or adjust

You don't fail because you're undisciplined. You fail because you haven't been taught the right way.

Let's fix that.

—-

⟐ The Golden Rule: Your Budget Should Match Your Life

Your budget must fit you, not the other way around.

Your income

Your responsibilities

Your lifestyle

Your values

Your habits

Your goals

Your culture
Your obligations
All of these matter.
A budget built for someone else will only frustrate you.

—-

◈ Building a Simple, Powerful Budget — Step-by-Step

1. Calculate Your Monthly Income
Include:
salary
business profit
side hustles
commissions
tips
remittances
passive income

Know your starting point.

—-

2. List ALL Your Expenses (Be Honest)
Break them into categories:
A) Essential Expenses

1. rent

1. transport

1. food

1. utilities

1. medical
1. school fees
1. debt repayment

B) Financial Goals

- savings
- investments
- SACCO contributions

C) Personal Needs & Lifestyle

- haircuts/salon
- clothing
- entertainment
- subscriptions
- gifting
- spiritual giving
- hobbies

D) Emergencies/Unexpected

- Small buffer fund

A realistic budget includes everything — including enjoyment.

—-

3. Use the 50/30/20 Rule (Flexible, Not Fixed)
50% — Needs (essentials)
30% — Wants (lifestyle)
20% — Savings & investments

If your income is small, adjust to:
70% needs
20% wants
10% savings

Or even:
80% needs
10% wants
10% savings

The percentage doesn't matter.
The consistency does.

—-

4. Allocate Every Shilling/Dollar

This is called zero-based budgeting. Every coin has a home. If you leave money homeless, it gets wasted.

Income – Expenses = 0

(Not zero spending — zero unassigned money.)

When your money has a purpose, you stop losing it to impulse habits.

—-

5. Track As You Go

You don't need fancy apps.

Use:

a small notebook
your phone notes
an envelope system
simple budgeting apps
Google Sheets

Tracking makes you aware. Awareness makes you powerful.

—-

6. Adjust Every Month

Your life changes. Your budget should too.

Review:

a. what worked

a. what didn't

a. where you overspent

a. where you underspent

a. what surprised you

a. what needs more funding

Budgeting is not a one-time event — it is a monthly conversation with your money.

—-

◈ Making Your Budget Work for You

1. Include Enjoyment

If your budget has no joy, you will rebel against it. Set aside something small for:

a treat
an outing
something you love
relaxation

A healthy budget supports your life — not suffocates it.

—-

2. Don't Aim for Perfection

You will slip.
You will make mistakes.
You will overspend sometimes.
It's normal.
Don't quit — adjust.
Budgeting is a skill.
You get better with practice.

—-

3. Protect Your Goals

Your savings and investments should be listed as expenses, not optional extras.

This makes them a priority, not a luxury.

—-

4. Build Accountability

Share your goals with:

a mentor
a trusted friend
a spouse
your SACCO group
your accountability partner

Support multiplies discipline.

—-

⍰ The Freedom a Budget Brings

Imagine:

No more end-of-month anxiety
Knowing exactly where your money goes
Being ahead of your bills
Saving consistently
Investing confidently
Having money left over
Seeing your goals getting funded
Sleeping peacefully
Being financially stable

Budgeting is not restriction. It is liberation.

It is the difference between surviving and rising.

—-

◈ **A Moment With You**

Close your eyes for a second.
Place your hand over your heart.
Whisper:
**"My money follows my direction.
I plan with purpose.
I am in control.
My budget is my compass — and it guides me to freedom."**
You are not managing money —
you are building a life.

◈ Chapter 12 — Building Financial Habits

"Small habits build big futures."

Habits are the quiet architects of your destiny.

Your financial life is not built in one big decision —it is built in tiny decisions repeated daily, weekly, monthly.

People often underestimate the power of small habits because they seem too simple... too ordinary... too easy.

But small habits compound.

Small habits create momentum.

Small habits shape character.

Small habits build wealth.

Your future is hiding inside your daily routines.

This chapter will guide you through building financial habits that are simple, repeatable, stabilizing — and deeply transformational.

—-

◈ Why Habits Matter More Than Motivation

Motivation feels exciting.

Habits feel ordinary.

Motivation starts the journey.

Habits finish it.

Motivation comes and goes.

Habits stay.

Motivation depends on emotion.

Habits depend on structure.

When you build financial habits, you no longer rely on "feeling inspired."

You move with discipline, clarity, and automatic consistency.

—-

◈ The Habit Loop That Builds Wealth

Every habit follows a simple cycle:

1. Cue – a reminder or trigger
2. Routine – the action you perform
3. Reward – the benefit you gain

When you design your habits intentionally, you turn wealth-building into a lifestyle, not a struggle.

Let's build your wealth loop.

—

◈ 10 Financial Habits That Change Everything

1. The Daily Expense Check (1–2 minutes)

Every evening, ask yourself:

What did I spend today?

Was it necessary?

How can I improve tomorrow?

This habit creates awareness — and awareness prevents waste.

—-

2. The Weekly Money Review

Every week:

update your budget

check your account balances

evaluate progress

adjust where needed

It keeps you honest and confident.

—-

3. The "Pay Yourself First" Habit

Every time money enters your hands — salary, business profit, gift — automatically take a portion and save or invest it before you spend.

Even if it's small:

$1

$5

KES 50

KES 200

Tiny amounts transform your future when repeated.

—-

4. Automate Your Savings

Set automatic transfers to:

SACCO

savings account

money market fund

investment account

Automation removes temptation.

You don't save what's left — you save first, then spend the rest.

—-

5. Consume Less, Create More

Instead of:

- **scrolling endlessly**
- **watching content**
- **comparing yourself**
- **overthinking**

Develop the habit of:

- **creating value**
- **learning new skills**
- **improving projects**
- **building your personal brand**
- **enhancing your mind**

Creators grow. Consumers remain stuck.

—-

6. Read or Listen to Something Financial Daily

Even 5 minutes is enough.

Read:

A page of a finance book

An article

A podcast

A thread

A tip

Your mind grows before your bank account does.

—-

7. The No-Spend Days

Choose 1–2 days per week where you intentionally spend nothing outside essentials.

No snacks.

No mobile money.

No spontaneous purchases.

This trains your discipline and slows down impulse spending.

—-

8. Review Subscriptions Monthly

Cancel what you don't use. People waste money on:

Forgotten apps

Unused gym memberships

Unnecessary bundles

Auto-renewals

This habit protects your pockets.

—-

9. Set Monthly Financial Goals

Write:

- One savings goal
- One spending goal
- One habit goal
- One learning goal

Every month.

Every month.

Every month.

This builds direction and momentum.

—-

10. Celebrate Your Progress

This is important.

Celebrate:

When you hit a target
When you pay off debt
When you save consistently
When you resist impulse spending
When you choose discipline

Celebration reinforces the behavior. Your brain repeats what feels rewarding.

—-

◈ Habit Stacking — The Secret Trick

The easiest way to build a new habit is to attach it to an existing one.

Examples:

After brushing teeth → review expenses
After morning prayer → read one finance page
After being paid → transfer savings
Every Sunday evening → weekly money review

Habits grow faster when linked to routines you already follow.

—-

◈ Start Small (This Is How Real Change Happens)

Don't aim for big habits. Aim for tiny habits that are impossible to fail.

Instead of:

"I'll save $100 a week." → Save $5 weekly.

"I'll read for 1 hour daily." → Read for 3 minutes.

"I'll never waste money again." → Track one expense daily.

Master tiny habits — then expand.

Small is sustainable.

Small becomes consistent.

Small creates change.

—-

◈ The Power of Consistency

Consistency is not perfection. Consistency means showing up even when:

You're tired

You're stressed

You're discouraged

You're busy

You're uninspired

You're unsure

Wealth does not come from one big move. It comes from small moves repeated endlessly.

Daily.

Weekly.

Monthly.

Quietly.

Faithfully.

Determinedly.

—-

⯑ Who You Become Through These Habits

When you practice financial habits consistently, you become:

Disciplined

Confident

Focused

Organized

Self-controlled

Intentional

Secure

Wise

Empowered

Your habits shape your identity. Your identity shapes your future.

You become the person wealthy people trust, follow, hire, and invest in.

—-

⯑ A Moment With You

Place your hand on your heart.

Take one deep breath.

Whisper:

"I am becoming disciplined.

I am becoming intentional.

I am building habits that build my future.

I am changing my life one small step at a time."

Small habits are not small.

They are seeds.

And seeds grow — always.

◈ Chapter 13 — Multiple Income Streams

"Never put your life in the hands of one income."

Relying on a single income is like relying on one leg to stand — you can balance for a while, but the moment life pushes you, you fall.

Financial independence requires stability. Stability requires diversification. Diversification requires multiple income streams.

Your salary can stop.

Your business can slow down.

The economy can shift.

Clients can disappear.

Health can fail.

Markets can change.

But if one stream dries up and you have others flowing, you stay standing.

This chapter will teach you how to create, grow, and maintain multiple income streams — no matter who you are, where you live, or what you currently earn.

—-

◈ Why One Income Is Too Risky

For years, society taught people:

"Get a job.

Earn a salary.

Live off it."

But the world changed.

Jobs are no longer guarantees.

Economies are unstable.

Technology shifts quickly.

Living costs rise faster than salaries.

Opportunities evolve rapidly.

Depending on one income is like tying your future to one rope — and hoping it never snaps.

We do not build wealth by hoping.

We build wealth by creating options.

—-

◈ The Misconception: "I need a lot of money to have multiple incomes."

This is false.

You don't need:

A big bank account, special connections, high education, expensive equipment, perfect timing

You only need:

- **Skills**
- **Willingness**
- **Consistency**
- **Self-belief**
- **Creativity**
- **Opportunity awareness**

Most multiple income streams start small, cheap, simple — and grow quietly.

—-

◈ The 7 Major Categories of Income Streams

You don't need all of these.

Start with one or two.
Grow slowly.
Expand naturally.

—-

1. Earned Income (Your job or main work)

This is your salary or primary hustle.
Most people stop at this one source —
but it is only the first stream, not the last. Use earned income to build the rest.

—-

2. Skill-Based Income

Money earned from your personal abilities:

freelancing
copywriting
graphic design
makeup artistry
hair styling
tutoring
baking
photography
digital marketing
repairing appliances
tailoring
social media management

This is the easiest and fastest stream to start.

—-

3. Product-Based Income

Selling something you can:

Create

Buy and resell

Package

Import

Supply

<u>Examples:</u>

Clothes

Beauty products

Supplements

Cakes/pastries

Stationery

Decor items

Food delivery

Thrift items

Handmade crafts

People are always buying something you only need to position yourself.

—-

4. Service-Based Income

You offer a service people need:

Cleaning

Babysitting

Virtual assistance

Laundry pickup/drop-off

Landscaping

Home repairs
Social media content
Event planning
Service businesses require very little capital — some require none.

—-

5. Passive Income

This is money that continues to flow after the initial work is done.
Examples:
Online courses
E-Books
Digital templates
Affiliate links
YouTube content
Monetized blogs
Royalties
Passive income grows slowly but becomes powerful over time.

—-

6. Investment Income

This is where true wealth begins.
Stocks
Bonds
SACCO dividends
Money market funds
Treasury bills
Real estate income
REITs
This stream grows silently, steadily, and consistently.

—-

7. Business Ownership

Owning or co-owning a business, even a small one, builds long-term financial security.

It could be:

A shop

A small salon

An online store

A food stall

A mobile business

A delivery service

A niche side company

Start small.

Improve slowly.

Just begin.

—-

<u>◈ The Secret: Don't Look for "the perfect idea" — Look for problems to solve</u>

Money flows toward solutions. Every time you notice:

A need

Agap

An inconvenience

A shortage

A complaint

A trend

A request

A repeated pattern

...you're looking at a potential income stream.

Wealthy people ask:

"What do people need that I can provide?"

Start asking the same.

—-

◈ How to Start Your First Income Stream

1. Identify what you already have

Ask yourself:

What am I good at?

What do people ask me to do?

What skill do I enjoy?

What comes naturally to me?

What do I know that others don't?

Your first income stream is usually already inside you.

—-

2. Start small

Don't wait until you're "ready."

Start:

with one client

with a small sample

with a test batch

with one sale

with one gig

with one attempt

Small beginnings are seeds for big outcomes.

—-

3. Use your networks

Tell people what you do.
Most opportunities come from:

1. Friends
2. Colleagues
3. Family
4. Online communities
5. Church groups
6. SACCOs
7. Neighbors

People cannot support you if they don't know what you offer.

—-

4. Improve your skills

Invest in learning through:
Free YouTube tutorials
Short online courses
Mentorship
Practice
Internships

Better skills → better income.

—-

5. Reinvest, don't consume

When money comes in from your side hustle:

1. Don't spend it

1. Don't upgrade lifestyle

1. Don't rush to splurge

Reinvest it to grow the stream. This is how small streams turn into rivers.

—-

◈ Protecting Your Energy: Managing Multiple Streams Wisely

Start with one.
Add the second when the first stabilizes.
Add the third when systems are in place.
Automate what you can.
Outsource when possible.
Maintain balance.
Avoid burnout.

Wealth is built through strategy, not chaos.

—-

◈ The Power of Having Options

When you have multiple income streams, you gain:

- Confidence
- Protection
- Peace
- Freedom

- Resilience
- Choice
- Strength

You stop living in fear of:

- Job loss
- Emergencies
- Bills
- Unexpected changes
- Economic instability

You stand firm no matter what.

—-

◈ A Moment With You

Close your eyes for a moment.
Take a deep breath.
Whisper:
"My life will not depend on one income.
I am creating options.
I am building streams.
I am opening doors.
My gifts shall make room for me."

You were never created to rely on just one source. You were created to flow — abundantly.

◈ Chapter 14 — Breaking Bad Money Habits

"Your future changes the moment your habits do."

Everyone wants financial freedom.

But not everyone wants to confront the habits that quietly sabotage it.

Bad money habits are like slow leaks you don't notice them at first, but over time, they drain your peace, your progress, and your potential.

This chapter is about facing your financial blind spots with honesty, courage, and grace... and replacing them with habits that build the future you desire.

No shame.

No guilt.

Just awareness, transformation, and elevation.

—-

◈ Why Bad Money Habits Are Hard to Break

Bad habits have roots:

Emotional roots
Childhood influences
Cultural expectations
Fear
Insecurity
Stress
Comparison
Lack of knowledge
Lack of role models

So don't judge yourself. Just understand yourself.

Once you understand why you do what you do, you can change what you do.

—-

⯑ 12 Bad Money Habits That Hold People Back (And How to Break Them)

—-

1. Impulse Spending

Buying things simply because they look nice, feel exciting, or offer temporary comfort.

Break it with:

The 48-hour rule

No-spend days

A shopping list

Controlled environments (don't browse "just to see")

Accountability

—-

2. Living for Approval

Buying things to impress, fit in, or look successful.

Break it with:

Defining your values

Setting financial goals

Practicing self-acceptance

Reducing comparison

The people who judge you won't pay your bills.

The people who love you don't care about your image.

—-

3. Not Tracking Money

If you don't track your money, it will wander — and get lost.

Break it with:

A weekly review

Simple apps or a small notebook

Daily awareness

Clarity is control.

—-

4. Spending First, Saving Last

Waiting until "whatever is left" to save — which often means nothing is left.

Break it with:

1. **Paying yourself first**
2. **Automating savings**

When savings become a priority, your future becomes a priority.

—-

5. Emotional Spending

Buying when lonely, stressed, bored, sad, or excited.

Break it with:

1. Identifying triggers

1. Alternative coping (journaling, walking, resting)

1. Delayed gratification

You cannot heal emotions with purchases.

—-

6. Borrowing for Non-Essentials

Taking loans for luxuries, outings, birthdays, fun, clothes, gadgets.

Break it with:

- **Only borrowing for emergencies or investments**
- **Building an emergency fund**
- **Learning delayed pleasure**

Debt steals tomorrow to pay for today.

—-

7. Ignoring Your Financial Reality

Avoiding checking balances, bills, or debts because it feels uncomfortable.

Break it with:

Weekly courage

Transparency with yourself

Facing the numbers

Avoidance increases fear. Awareness decreases it.

—-

8. Depending on Others Financially

Relying on someone else's money — friends, relatives, partners — instead of creating your own strength.

Break it with:

- **Building skills**
- **Starting small hustles**
- **Planning your own goals**

Dependency creates limitations. Independence creates power.

—-

9. Saying "Yes" to Everyone

Helping others financially even when it hurts your own stability.

Break it with:

- **Boundaries**
- **Polite firmness**
- **Planned generosity**

You cannot pour from an empty cup.

10. Trying to Look Rich Instead of Becoming Rich

Chasing the image of wealth instead of the substance.

Break it with:

- **Simple living**
- **Focusing on growth**
- **Valuing peace over appearances**

Let your success be felt, not flaunted.

—-

11. Consuming More Than You Learn
Endless scrolling, entertainment, and distraction with no growth.
Break it with:
dedicating 10 minutes a day to learning

- Reading financial content
- Joining a SACCO or growth community

Knowledge compounds faster than money.

—-

12. Treating Money Casually
No plan.
No strategy.
No goals.
Just vibes.
Break it with:

- **Budgeting**

- **Intentionality**
- **Vision setting**

Money respects those who respect it.

—-

⟐ The Transformation Process: How to Replace Bad Habits With Better Ones

Breaking bad habits is not about force.
It's about design.
Here's the process:

—-

1. Identify the Root

Ask:
Why do I do this?
What emotion drives it?
What triggers it?
What am I trying to feel?

The habit is the fruit. The emotion is the root.

—-

2. Replace, Don't Remove

Don't just stop spending emotionally —
replace it with:
Journaling

Calling a friend
Walking
Resting
Reading
Praying
Breathing

Replacement is easier than removal.

—-

3. Create Friction
Make bad habits harder:

- **Delete shopping apps**
- **Remove auto-fill payment details**
- **Leave bank cards at home**
- **Avoid tempting environments**

The harder it is to do, the easier it is to stop.

—-

4. Reward Good Behaviors
Celebrate when you:
Save
Resist temptation
Stick to your budget

Make a wise decision

Your brain repeats what it feels rewarded for.

—-

5. Track Your Progress

Small wins matter. Write them down.
Progress builds identity.
Identity builds confidence.
Confidence builds momentum.

—-

◈ The New You: A Person of Discipline

When you break your bad money habits, you become:

- Clearer
- Stronger
- Calmer
- More confident
- More responsible
- More focused
- More self-aware

You begin to trust yourself.

Your future becomes stable.
Your money obeys you.

—-

⟐ A Moment With You

Place your hand over your heart.
Close your eyes.
Say softly:
"I release my old habits.
I choose discipline.
I choose wisdom.
I choose transformation.
My future is changing because I am changing."
Bad habits do not define you. But your new habits will refine you.

⯑ Chapter 15 — Discipline

"Discipline is the bridge between wanting wealth and becoming wealthy."

Everyone wants financial freedom. But wanting is not enough. Dreaming is not enough. Planning is not enough. Even knowledge is not enough.

What separates the financially free from the financially frustrated is one thing:

Discipline.

Discipline is the quiet force that shapes your destiny. It is the strength to choose long-term peace over short-term pleasure.

It is the ability to remain focused even when motivation disappears. It is doing what is necessary — especially when you do not feel like it.

This chapter will show you how to develop the kind of discipline that keeps your goals alive, your habits strong, and your future secure.

—-

⯑ Discipline Is a Skill, Not a Personality Trait

Some people think:

"I'm just not a disciplined person."

Or

"Discipline is for the strict and serious."

But discipline is not something you are born with. It is something you build.

No one wakes up naturally disciplined they train it through decisions, repetition, and structure.

You are not "bad with money." You simply need systems that support your goals.

Discipline is available to you.

—-

⟐ What Discipline Really Means

Discipline is not punishment.
Discipline is not restriction.
Discipline is not deprivation.
Discipline is:
Consistency
Clarity
Decision
Direction
Self-control
Intention
Strength
Structure

Discipline is freedom in disguise.

—-

⟐ Why Discipline Is the Greatest Wealth-Building Tool

Money grows for the disciplined.
Opportunities open for the disciplined.
Peace belongs to the disciplined.
Discipline ensures that:
You stick to your budget
You remain consistent in your savings
You invest regularly
You avoid unnecessary spending
You progress in your career
You build strong habits
You grow multiple income streams

You protect your financial goals
You don't quit when life gets hard

Discipline is the engine of financial independence.

—-

◈ The 6 Pillars of Financial Discipline

—-

1. Clear Goals
You cannot be disciplined without a target.
Ask yourself:
What am I working toward?
What do I want in 1 year? 3 years? 5 years?
What does financial freedom look like for me?

Your goals guide your discipline.

—-

2. Daily Structure
Discipline thrives in routine.
This includes:
Morning habits
Budgeting habits
Accountability habits
Spending rules
Saving systems

Structure reduces emotional decisions.

—-

3. Consistency Over Intensity

It is better to:

Save small amounts consistently

Invest regularly at any pace

Study 10 minutes a day

Improve steadily

Consistency beats perfection every time.

—-

4. Delayed Gratification

This is the heart of discipline.

It is choosing:

1. Savings over impulse

1. Investing over show-off spending

1. Peace over validation

1. Long-term goals over short-term excitement

Discipline is quiet. But its rewards speak loudly.

—-

5. Accountability

You become stronger when someone checks on your progress.
This could be:
A mentor
A trusted friend
A financial advisor
Your SACCO group
A partner

Accountability multiplies discipline.

—-

6. Emotional Control

Money and emotions are deeply connected.

Discipline requires recognizing when your emotions try to take over:

- Stress
- Boredom
- Loneliness
- Insecurity
- Pressure
- Excitement

When your emotions lead, your wallet bleeds.
When discipline leads, your future succeeds.

—-

<u>◈ How to Build Discipline Naturally (Without Forcing It)</u>

—-

1. Start With One Habit

Don't overwhelm yourself.
Pick one thing:

Track spending
Save weekly
Avoid impulse purchases
Study a new skill
Follow a budget

Do it until it becomes automatic.

—-

2. Build Your Environment, Not Your Willpower

Willpower fades. Environment shapes you.

Remove temptations
Limit exposure to unnecessary shopping
Keep savings inaccessible
Use cash envelopes
Automate important financial actions

Your environment should support your goals.

—-

3. Reward Yourself

Don't associate discipline with suffering.
Celebrate your wins:

A small treat

A relaxing day
Buying something meaningful
Acknowledging your progress

Reward reinforces effort.

—-

4. Track Your Success

Write down:
What you saved
What you invested
What habits you kept
What temptations you resisted

Seeing your progress builds discipline in your soul.

—-

5. Forgive Yourself When You Slip

You will make mistakes.
You will overspend occasionally.
You will break your routines sometimes.
Don't punish yourself.
Don't quit.
Just reset and continue.
Success belongs to those who restart without shame.

—-

◈ The Identity of a Disciplined Person

Discipline is not just what you do.

It becomes part of who you are.

A disciplined person:

Thinks before spending

Plans before acting

Invests consistently

Saves automatically

Learns continuously

Works steadily

Holds themselves accountable

Sees the bigger picture

You begin to carry a quiet confidence. People trust you. Opportunities find you. Money flows to you. Life respects you.

—-

◈ A Moment With You

Close your eyes and take a deep breath.

Whisper:

"My future is worth the discipline.

My dreams are worth the effort.

My life is worth the structure.

I choose consistency.

I choose growth.

I choose discipline."

This is the chapter where your transformation deepens.

Your wealth is not built in your hands it is built in your habits. And discipline is the architect behind it all.

◈ Chapter 16 — Health & Wealth

"Your body is the engine of your financial future — protect it."

You can build income streams, study new skills, save faithfully, invest wisely, and work hard... but if your health collapses, everything else collapses with it.

Financial independence is not only about money. It is about strength, clarity, energy, stability, and ability.

Your health is your first capital.

Your body is your first investment.

Your well-being is your first wealth.

This chapter is a reminder that you cannot chase financial freedom while neglecting the vessel that carries you toward it.

—-

◈ Why Your Health Is Part of Your Wealth Strategy

People often separate health and finances — but they are deeply connected.

Poor health leads to: missed work, lower productivity, reduced creativity, stress and anxiety, medical bills, burnout, emotional instability, lost opportunities, and slow career progression

Good health leads to:

higher focus
more energy
stronger decision-making
better mood
clarity in planning
increased earning potential
consistency in goals

lower medical expenses

A healthy you is a more powerful you.

—-

◈ 5 Areas of Health That Affect Your Wealth

1. Physical Health

Your body must sustain your dreams.

Poor physical health reduces: energy, stamina, resilience, focus, and discipline

Taking care of your physical body is not luxury — it's responsibility.

Key habits:

✓ drink water consistently

✓ walk daily

✓ eat balanced meals

✓ avoid excessive sugar/fast food

✓ sleep enough

✓ stretch

✓ schedule check-ups

✓ practice safe habits

Your body is your engine. Keep it running smoothly.

—-

2. Mental & Emotional Health

An exhausted mind cannot think clearly. A stressed mind cannot plan. A depressed mind cannot see possibility. An anxious mind cannot take risks. A worried mind cannot grow wealth.

<u>Protect your emotional well-being by:</u>

- resting intentionally
- journaling
- taking breaks from social media
- praying or meditating
- talking through pain & pressure
- limiting draining relationships
- practicing self-compassion

Your mental clarity shapes your financial clarity.

—-

3. Spiritual Health

A spiritually grounded person is:

a. centered

a. hopeful

a. purposeful

a. stable

a. guided

a. resilient

a. calm

Spiritual health gives you a sense of meaning, direction, and inner peace.

It reminds you that:

- your journey is supported
- your purpose is bigger than your fear
- your strength is not your own
- your blessings have divine guidance

Spiritual grounding strengthens every financial decision.

—-

4. Social Health

Your relationships influence:

a. your confidence

a. your habits

a. your spending

a. your decisions

a. your exposure to opportunities

Healthy connections help you rise. Toxic connections drain you financially, mentally, and emotionally.

Choose wisely.

—-

5. Financial Stress Management

Financial stress affects your:

- Sleep
- Blood pressure
- Mood
- Relationships
- Immune system
- Decision-making

This is why building emergency funds, budgeting, saving, and planning matters — not just for money, but for peace.

—-

⟐ The Hidden Costs of Neglecting Your Health

When you ignore your health, the bill arrives later — and it's always expensive.

Financially expensive.

Emotionally expensive.

Physically expensive.

Relationally expensive.

Prevention is always cheaper than crisis. Take care of yourself early, and consistently.

—-

⟐ The Wealth Habits of Healthy People

Healthy people:

a. prioritize rest

a. maintain boundaries

a. know when to pause

a. nourish their bodies

a. refresh their minds

a. move regularly

a. practice gratitude

a. say "no" wisely

a. seek help when needed

a. keep their stress low

a. manage their emotional world

These habits directly increase their capacity to earn, grow, and thrive.

—-

◈ Self-Care as a Financial Strategy

Self-care isn't indulgence.
Self-care is maintenance.
Self-care is discipline.
Self-care is preparation.
You cannot pour into your future from a drained vessel.
A well-rested you: makes better decisions.
A mentally stable you: handles money wisely.
A spiritually anchored you: remains steady in storms.
A physically energized you: finishes what you start.

—-

◈ Practical Ways to Strengthen Your Health for Wealth

1. Schedule Rest Like a Meeting

Don't rest when you break down. Rest to prevent breaking down.

—-

2. Move Your Body Daily

Even 10 minutes changes your energy, mood, and clarity.

—-

3. Eat for Fuel, Not Emotion

Your body needs nourishment, not punishment or neglect.

—-

4. Protect Your Sleep

Sleep is a natural reset button.

—-

5. Reduce Digital Overload

You don't need to consume everything the world offers.

—-

6. Set Boundaries

Not every request, message, or expectation needs your energy.

—-

7. Seek Peaceful Spaces

Nature, quiet moments, prayer, meditation — these are free, powerful, and healing.

—-

8. Laugh More

Joy strengthens your health and lightens your mind.

—-

9. Build Supportive Friendships

People who uplift you amplify your potential.

—-

10. Practice Gratitude

A thankful heart is a wealthy heart.

—-

◈ A Moment With You

Place your hand gently on your chest.
Close your eyes.
Whisper slowly:
"My health is my wealth.
My body is blessed.
My mind is clear.
My spirit is strong.
I will protect the vessel that carries my destiny."
A strong future requires a strong you.

⟐ Chapter 17 — Mentorship & Community

"Success accelerates when you stop walking alone."

You can walk far by yourself — but you will walk faster, smarter, and more confidently when you walk with the right people.

Financial independence is not a solo journey. Yes, you make your own decisions. Yes, you take responsibility for your habits. Yes, you shape your own future. But the truth is this:

You rise faster when you learn from those who have walked the path before you.

And you stay consistent when you surround yourself with people who are rising too.

Welcome to the chapter that transforms your journey from isolated effort to collective elevation.

—-

⟐ Why You Need Mentorship

A mentor is not necessarily someone wealthy or famous. A mentor is someone who sees further than you, knows more than you, and helps you avoid mistakes they already made.

A mentor gives you:

Perspective
Clarity
Guidance
Accountability
Wisdom
Encouragement
Shortcuts
Correction
Confidence

A mentor is a mirror, a map, and a voice of direction.

—-

◈ The 3 Types of Mentors You Need

1. Skill Mentor

Someone who teaches you how to:

Become better at your craft

Grow in your career

Improve your business

Master industry knowledge

Sharpen your abilities

They help you earn more through competence.

—-

2. Financial Mentor

Someone who guides you on: saving, investing, budgeting, handling credit, understanding money and building wealth. They help you avoid costly financial mistakes.

—-

3. Life Mentor

Someone who supports your overall growth: character, mindset, choices, relationships, boundaries, and spiritual development. They help you stay grounded, balanced, and wise.

—-

Mentors expand your world. They stretch your thinking. They open doors your effort alone could not open.

—-

◈ How to Find a Mentor

You don't have to wait for a mentor to appear magically. You can intentionally seek one out.

Look for someone who:

- Has the results you desire
- Has integrity
- Communicates clearly
- Is consistent
- Is willing to teach
- Has a generous heart
- Wants to see others grow

A mentor can be: a supervisor, a colleague, a business owner, a family friend, an elder in your community, a spiritual leader, a financial expert, a successful entrepreneur, a coach, a writer, podcaster, or online teacher

Mentorship does not always require physical presence — guidance can come through books, courses, audio lessons, or online groups.

—-

◈ How to Be a Good Mentee

Mentorship is a two-way relationship.
To benefit fully:

1. Be teachable
1. Ask questions
1. Show respect
1. Take notes
1. Follow through on advice
1. Be consistent
1. Show appreciation
1. Don't waste their time
1. Come prepared
1. Be honest about your challenges

The more you commit to growth, the more your mentor invests in you.

—-

◈ The Power of Community

You rise faster when surrounded by people who are rising too.
Your financial community might include:

SACCOs
Investment clubs
Saving groups
Professional networks
Business circles
Accountability partners
Faith communities
Personal growth groups

<u>A strong community gives you:</u>

- Encouragement
- Opportunities
- Shared learning
- Collaboration
- Referrals
- Exposure
- Support during challenges
- A sense of belonging

Community keeps you accountable.
Community keeps you motivated.
Community keeps you grounded.

—-

◈ The Wrong Community Can Destroy Your Progress

Not everyone around you shares your goals.

Not everyone wants to grow.

Not everyone is disciplined.

Not everyone is wise with money.

Be careful with people who:

Encourage reckless spending

Mock your goals

Borrow without returning

Compete instead of support

Gossip instead of grow

Distract instead of elevate

Drain your peace

Push you into debt

You become like the people you surround yourself with.

Choose wisely.

Choose intentionally.

Choose people who reflect your future, not your past.

—-

◈ How to Build a Financial Growth Circle

Start simple:

Find 2–4 people who want to grow.

Set monthly goals together.

Share resources and ideas.

Hold each other accountable.

Create a saving or investing plan.

Celebrate wins and progress.

A small group with vision is more powerful than a large group with no direction.

—-

◈Collaboration: The Secret Accelerator

One of the fastest ways to grow is to collaborate, not compete.

Collaborate on: business ideas, side hustles, partnerships, skill-sharing, study groups, financial planning, accountability challenges

Where there is unity, there is acceleration.

—-

◈ A Moment With You

Place your hand on your heart.

Close your eyes.

Whisper:

"I am not walking alone.

I am surrounded by wisdom.

My community is rising.

My mentors guide me.

I am supported, strengthened, and aligned."

You are not climbing this mountain by yourself. You are supported. You are guided. You are becoming. And the people you walk with will shape who you become next.

◈ Chapter 18 — Identity & Self-Belief

"You cannot build a wealthy life with a poor identity."

You can learn every wealth strategy. You can collect every financial book. You can save, invest, budget, and plan. You can chase opportunities and work hard...

But if deep inside you believe:

"I'm not good enough,"

"I don't deserve wealth,"

"I'm not smart with money,"

"People like me don't succeed,"

"I'll always struggle,"

"My background limits me,"

...then your financial life will always shrink to match your inner identity.

Identity is the thermostat of your life. Even if opportunities raise the temperature, if your self-belief is low, you will unconsciously turn the heat back down.

This chapter is about raising your internal temperature — your self-worth, your vision, your sense of possibility.

Because wealth starts inside you long before it manifests around you.

—-

◈ Identity Shapes Destiny

Identity is:

How you see yourself

What you believe you deserve

What you believe is possible

What you believe you can handle

What you believe you can create

Your outer life is simply a reflection of your inner beliefs. People don't rise because they have money. People rise because they have belief.

—-

◈ How a Weak Identity Sabotages Wealth

A weak identity leads to:

1. Self-sabotage
1. Procrastination
1. Fear of risk
1. Fear of success
1. Fear of responsibility
1. Low standards
1. Poor financial decisions
1. Settling for less
1. Staying in comfort zones
1. Avoiding opportunities

<u>Because deep inside, you may feel:</u> unworthy, insecure, afraid,unsure, undeserving

And your actions will match those feelings.

—-

◈ **A Strong Identity Creates Wealth**

People who believe in themselves:

Pursue opportunities

Take courageous steps

Invest early

Ask questions

Surround themselves with mentors

Grow new skills

Make bold decisions

Set higher standards

Persist longer

Accept abundance

A strong identity makes wealth natural.

—-

◈ **Rewrite the Story You Tell Yourself**

Your past is a chapter, not a prophecy.

Maybe you grew up in poverty. Maybe you were mocked. Maybe you failed. Maybe you struggled. Maybe you made financial mistakes. Maybe you've never seen anyone succeed. But now you get to write a new story.

Say this aloud, gently:

"I am becoming the person my future needs."

Identity is not fixed. Identity is chosen.

—-

⟐ Who Are You Becoming?

Start describing the future you — not with fear, but with faith.

Describe yourself as:

- **disciplined**
- **wise**
- **consistent**
- **responsible**
- **focused**
- **confident**
- **secure**
- **creative**
- **resourceful**
- **teachable**
- **patient**
- **forward-thinking**
- **financially aware**
- **spiritually anchored**

Your words shape your identity.
Your identity shapes your results.

—-

⟐ The Power of Self-Belief

Self-belief is not arrogance. It is alignment with your potential.
Self-belief is knowing:

- "I can learn."
- "I can grow."
- "I can rise."
- "I can change my story."
- "I can build wealth."
- "I can handle responsibility."
- "I can become more."

Self-belief is the currency that opens doors before money does.

—-

⟐ How to Strengthen Your Identity

1. Change Your Inner Language

Stop saying:

- "I'm bad with money."

- "I'm always broke."
- "I can't save."
- "This is too hard."
- "I don't know enough."

Replace with:

- "I am learning."
- "I am improving."
- "I am becoming disciplined."
- "I am growing wiser every day."
- "I am becoming financially strong."

Your words reprogram your path.

—-

2. Surround Yourself With Believing People

People who see your potential help you rise into it.

If you stay around people who doubt you, you will eventually doubt yourself.

—-

3. Track Your Progress

Every small win strengthens your identity:

saving even a little

learning a new skill

saying no to impulse spending

investing consistently

growing professionally

Proof builds belief.

—-

4. Break One Limiting Belief at a Time

Pick one belief to challenge:

"I don't deserve wealth."

"Money is too hard."

"People like me don't succeed."

Prove it wrong through action — 1% improvement each day.

—-

5. Heal Your Relationship With Money

Some people fear money because of past pain.

Forgive yourself for: past mistakes, past debt, past losses, past struggles

You were learning.

Now you're rising.

—-

6. Build Your Spiritual Identity

A spiritually grounded identity is powerful.

It believes:

Provision is possible

Progress is possible

Transformation is possible

Destiny is possible

Abundance is possible

Faith fuels identity.

—-

◈ Identity and Wealth Are Twins

You cannot sustain what your identity cannot hold. If you don't believe in yourself, you will sabotage your progress.

If you believe you are limited, your life will reflect that limitation. But once you raise your identity, everything in your life rises with it:

Your habits

Your decisions

Your standards

Your income

Your goals

Your relationships

Your future

Your identity is the soil. Wealth is the harvest.

—-

◈ A Moment With You

Place both hands over your chest.
Close your eyes.
Whisper slowly:
"I am worthy of abundance.
I am capable of growth.
I am becoming stronger.
I am becoming wiser.
I am becoming the wealthiest version of myself — inside and out."
Wealth begins inside you.
And now, you are ready to embody it.

⟐ Chapter 19 — Money & Relationships

"Money reveals the truth about relationships — and about ourselves."

Money does not destroy relationships it exposes them.

It exposes:

Values

Priorities

Habits

Boundaries

Trust

Maturity

Intentions

Responsibility

Character

How people handle money reveals how they handle life. And because relationships deeply affect your finances, this chapter will help you navigate love, family, friendships, and partnerships with wisdom and clarity.

—-

⟐ Why Money and Relationships Are Connected

Your financial life does not exist in isolation.

The people around you influence:

- ❖ how you spend
- ❖ how you save
- ❖ how you invest

- ❖ how you plan
- ❖ how you think
- ❖ how you feel about money

Relationships can either accelerate your financial growth or silently drain your potential.

The goal is not to cut people off blindly.

The goal is to build healthy boundaries, shared values, and mutual respect.

—-

◈ 4 Types of Relationships That Shape Your Financial Journey

1. Romantic Relationships

Love is beautiful —

but unmanaged money can turn love into frustration.

<u>A strong financial relationship involves:</u>

Honesty
Shared goals
Transparency
Teamwork
Accountability
Planning
Respect

Couples thrive when they discuss:

✓ Spending habits

✓ Savings goals

✓ Debt

✓ Budgeting styles

✓ Career ambitions

✓ Money fears

✓ Personal financial history

✓ Long-term visions

Love cannot survive where money is a secret. Transparency keeps love strong.

—-

2. Family
Family can be supportive — or draining, depending on dynamics.
Common financial pressures from family include:

- Requests for money
- Emotional manipulation
- Expectations to provide
- Cultural obligations
- Guilt
- Comparison

- Entitlement

You must learn how to say:

"No, not this time."

"I can't afford that."

"I need to prioritize my future right now."

Helping family is good — but sacrificing your stability to meet their demands is not.

Healthy giving comes from abundance, not pressure.

—-

3. Friends

Friends influence your financial habits more than you realize.

<u>With the wrong friends:</u>

★ You overspend

★ You live for approval

★ You feel pressured

★ You make emotional decisions

★ You chase trends

★ You fear being "different"

<u>But with the right friends:</u>

1. You save together

1. Invest together

1. Share opportunities

1. Exchange knowledge

1. Encourage each other

1. Hold each other accountable

1. Grow together

Your friendships should match your direction, not your distractions.

—-

4. Professional & Business Partnerships
Money reveals integrity. Be cautious of people who:

★ Avoid transparency

★ Dislike documentation

★ Pressure you to invest quickly

★ Lack consistency

★ Actt secretive

★ Overpromise

★ Resist accountability

Great partnerships are built on:

- Trust
- Clarity
- Communication
- Written agreements
- Defined roles
- Shared vision
- Mutual benefit

Partnerships can multiply your wealth or multiply your problems. Choose wisely.

—-

◈ The Most Dangerous Money Dynamics

1. Being Everyone's Financial Savior

If you allow people to rely on you for every crisis, you will become their solution instead of helping them create their own.

Learn to help without enabling.

—-

2. Borrowing to Impress People

Trying to look successful to people who aren't paying your bills is financial suicide.

—-

3. Staying Silent About Money in Relationships

Silence creates assumptions.
Assumptions create conflict.
Conflict creates resentment.
Communicate early and often.

—-

4. Comparing Your Finances to Others

Comparison creates pressure, pressure leads to poor decisions.
Run your own race.

—-

5. Mixing Money With People Who Lack Integrity

No amount of potential profit is worth partnering with someone who cannot be trusted.

—-

◈ Healthy Money Boundaries

Boundaries protect your peace, your progress, and your purpose.
Healthy boundaries include:

- Saying no without guilt
- Setting financial limits
- Being honest about what you can afford
- Not lending more than you can lose
- Not letting others guilt-trip you

- Protecting your savings
- Being mindful of shared expenses
- Choosing growth-minded relationships

Boundaries are not selfish. They are self-respect.

—-

◈ Creating Shared Financial Vision in Romantic Relationships

A financially healthy relationship includes:

1. Shared goals

★ Building a home

★ Investing

★ Saving

★ Starting a business

★ Creating an emergency fund

2. Joint planning

Dream together.
Budget together.
Review progress together.

3. Transparency

Be open about:

- income
- debt
- expenses
- fears
- ambitions

Secrets destroy trust. Honesty builds unity.

4. Teamwork

Money should unite, not divide.

—-

◈ Healing Your Relationship With Money

Your personal relationship with money affects every other relationship too.

Ask yourself:

1. **Do I use money to impress others?**
1. **Do I fear losing money?**
1. **Do I avoid money conversations?**
1. **Do I feel unworthy of wealth?**
1. **Do I associate money with pain or stress?**

Healing begins with recognition.
Transformation begins with intention.

—-

◈ How to Protect Your Financial Journey From Negative Influence

—-

1. Reduce Access
Not everyone deserves insight into your financial life.

—-

2. Limit Emotional Spending Influences
Some people trigger your need to "keep up."
Distance yourself until you gain strength.

—-

3. Set Clear Boundaries
Communicate respectfully but firmly.

—-

4. Build a Supportive Financial Circle
Choose people with discipline, wisdom, and ambition.

—-

5. Choose a Vision-Aligned Partner
Your partner should grow with you, not drain you.

—-

◈ A Moment With You

Close your eyes.

Breathe deeply.

Whisper:

"I protect my peace.

I choose relationships that nurture my growth.

I walk with people who walk with wisdom.

My journey is blessed, supported, and aligned."

You don't need to walk alone. But you must choose carefully who walks beside you.

◈ Chapter 20 — Entrepreneurship

"Businesses are built by ordinary people who dare to solve problems."

Entrepreneurship is not about being extraordinary.

It's not about being talented, lucky, or born into the right family.

It's about seeing a problem and deciding to solve it — consistently, creatively, and courageously.

Every great business began with a simple question:

"How can I help?"

"What do people need that they're not getting yet?"

"What solution can I bring to this community?"

Entrepreneurship is a mindset before it becomes a business.

This chapter will help you step into that mindset with clarity, confidence, and purpose.

—-

◈ The Mindset of an Entrepreneur

Before you start a business, you must become a business-minded person.

Entrepreneurs think differently:

1. They see opportunities, not obstacles.

1. They solve problems, not complain about them.

1. They take calculated risks, not reckless leaps.

1. They focus on service, not applause.

1. They grow through challenges, not run from them.

1. They learn constantly, not stagnate

1. They believe in their ability to create value.

Entrepreneurship is not just about money — it's about becoming someone who brings solutions to the world.

—-

⟐ The Truth: You Don't Need Big Capital to Start

Many people never start because they think:
"I need a lot of money."
"I need a big space."
"I need fancy equipment."
"I need everything to be perfect."
No.
You need resourcefulness, not resources.
Most great entrepreneurs started with:
Small capital
Borrowed tools
Home-based operations
Simple ideas
One customer
One skill
One step

Start small.
Grow steadily.
Expand intelligently.

—-

⟐ How to Find a Profitable Business Idea

The best business ideas come from:

1. Solving Problems

1. What frustrates people?
2. What do people complain about?
3. What is missing?

Where there is pain, there is profit.

—-

2. Using Your Skills

What are you naturally good at?

Examples:

Cooking
Organizing
Design
Writing
Teaching
Repairing
Cleaning
Crafting

Your skill can become someone's solution.

—-

3. Filling Gaps in Your Community

Look around:

1. **What do people wish they had?**

1. **What service is missing?**

1. **What product is needed?**

Simple gaps create strong businesses.

—-

4. Passion + Demand

Your passion matters — but passion must meet demand.
Ask:
"Do people need this?"
"Will they pay for it?"
Where passion and demand meet, business thrives.

—-

<u>◈ Types of Businesses You Can Start (Even With Little Capital)</u>

1. Online services (design, writing, VA work)
2. Beauty services (hair, nails, makeup)
3. Food services (baking, meal prep, delivery)
4. Cleaning services
5. Tutoring or teaching
6. Digital products
7. Social media management
8. Small-scale trading
9. Delivery services
10. Repair services
11. Thrifting / resale
12. Farming or home gardening
13. Content creation
14. Event planning
15. Photography

The options are endless. Your creativity is your capital.

—-

◈ The 5 Pillars of a Successful Business

1. Value

Your business must help people in a real way.

—-

2. Customer Service

Customers remember how you made them feel.

Be:

Respectful

Reliable

Honest

Consistent

Good service builds loyalty. Loyalty builds income.

—-

3. Quality

Even if you start small, start with excellence.

Quality builds reputation. Reputation builds growth.

—-

4. Consistency

Show up when you feel like it.

Show up when you don't.

Show up whether business is slow or fast.

Consistency builds momentum.

—-

5. Smart Financial Management

Separate your business money from your personal money.

Track:

Income

Expenses

Stock

Profit

Losses

A business that is not tracked is a business that won't last.

—-

◈ The Entrepreneur's Challenges (And How to Overcome Them)

1. Fear

Fear of failure.

Fear of judgment.

Fear of losing money.

Fear of trying something new.

Solution: Start anyway — fear shrinks through action.

—-

2. Slow Progress

Businesses take time to grow.

Solution: Be consistent, patient, and strategic.

—-

3. Competition

Don't fear competition — it means there is demand.

Solution: Offer value and a unique experience.

—-

4. Mistakes

You will make mistakes.

Every entrepreneur does.

Solution: Learn quickly. Adjust. Grow.

—-

5. Burnout

You cannot pour from an empty cup.

Solution: Rest, plan, delegate, simplify.

—-

◈ How to Grow a Business Once It Starts

1. Reinvent and improve constantly

Don't stay the same — evolve.

2. Market wisely

Tell people what you offer.

Use social media.

Use word of mouth.

Show your work.

3. Build relationships

Business grows through people.

4. Keep learning

Study marketing, finance, customer psychology, and industry trends.

5. Track your numbers

What you measure improves.

6. Reinvest profits

Don't eat your seed. Reinvest to grow.

—-

◈The Spiritual Side of Entrepreneurship

Entrepreneurship requires:
Prayer
Faith
Patience
Humility
Perseverance
Gratitude

You will have days when nothing works — and days when everything works.

Both seasons teach you.
Both seasons grow you.
Both seasons refine you.
Stay grounded.
Stay aligned.
Stay guided.

—-

◈ A Moment With You

Close your eyes.
Breathe in deeply.
Whisper softly:
"I am a creator of solutions.
I am capable of building something meaningful.
My ideas matter.
My gifts matter.
My business will grow,
because I am growing."
Entrepreneurship is not for the perfect.
It is for the courageous.

And you are courageous.

◈ Chapter 21 — Long-Term Wealth Strategy

"Wealth doesn't respond to speed; it responds to consistency."

Real wealth is not built in a moment — it is built through rhythms, decisions, disciplines, and systems that compound over time.

Many people want wealth fast.

Few are willing to build it right.

But long-term wealth is not a magic formula — it is a lifestyle.

This chapter will help you create a financial strategy that grows quietly, steadily, and powerfully, year after year.

—-

◈ The Difference Between Getting Rich Fast and Building Wealth Slowly

Getting rich fast depends on:

1. Luck
2. Trends
3. Hype
4. Timing
5. Risk
6. Temporary momentum

Building wealth slowly depends on:

Wisdom

Planning

Patience

Consistency

Discipline

Long-term thinking
Fast riches are unstable. Slow wealth is unshakeable.

—-

◈ The 3 Stages of Long-Term Wealth

1. Foundation
This is where you build:
Discipline
Budgeting skills
Saving habits
Emergency funds
Financial awareness
This stage is not glamorous. But without it, nothing stands.

—-

2. Growth
This is where you:

- **Increase your income**
- **Add new skills**
- **Pursue promotions**
- **Start businesses**
- **Develop multiple income streams**
- **Invest consistently**

This stage expands your earning potential.

—-

3. Expansion
This is where your money begins to multiply itself.
You focus on:

- **Investments**
- **Passive income**
- **Long-term assets**
- **Land**
- **Real estate**
- **Stocks**
- **Shares**
- **Partnerships**
- **Wealth protection**

This stage creates generational change. You do not have to rush through these stages. Grow steadily. Grow wisely. Grow intentionally.

—-

◈The 7 Pillars of Long-Term Wealth

1. Continuous Learning

The financially wise never stop learning.

Study:

- Money
- Investing
- Business
- Your career field
- Personal development
- Financial markets
- Leadership
- Communication

Knowledge compounds like money —
quietly, but powerfully.

—-

2. Income Growth

You cannot build long-term wealth with a stagnant income.

Increase your earning power by:

Upskilling
Negotiating your salary
Learning in-demand skills
Taking certifications
Changing career paths
Starting side hustles
Freelancing
Entrepreneurship
Networking intentionally

The more you earn, the more you can build.

—-

3. Consistent Saving

Not saving occasionally — saving consistently, automatically.

Saving teaches you discipline, stability, and control. Your future self will thank you.

—-

4. Smart Investing

Investing is where wealth multiplies. Choose long-term investments like:

Index funds
Government bonds
Mutual funds
Retirement plans
Real estate

Dividend-paying stocks
SACCO investments
Low-risk long-term shares
Invest slowly, steadily, without panic.

—-

5. Debt Management

You cannot walk into wealth while dragging chains.
Clear harmful debt.
Avoid unnecessary debt.
Use debt responsibly and strategically if needed.
Debt is not evil — mismanaged debt is.

—-

6. Asset Building

Wealth grows when you own things that appreciate.
Assets include:
Land
Real estate
Intellectual property
Businesses
Investments
Stocks
Equipment
Digital assets
Buy things that gain value over time.

—-

7. Protection

Protect what you build through:
Emergency funds

Insurance
Legal documents
Boundaries
Wise partners
Careful planning

Wealth is not only about growth — it's also about preservation.

—-

◈ Compounding: The Quiet Miracle of Wealth

Compounding is the force that grows wealth slowly at first... then suddenly.

It is the reason:

- Small investments become large
- Consistent savings turn into safety
- Slow growth becomes unstoppable
- Time becomes your greatest ally

Compounding rewards those who start early and stay consistent.

—-

◈ 10 Long-Term Wealth Habits to Practice Daily

Live below your means
Increase your income annually
Save automatically

Invest monthly
Track your expenses
Avoid impulsive spending
Set annual financial goals
Review your progress quarterly
Diiversify your income
Practice patience

These habits look simple — but together, they build extraordinary futures.

—-

◈ The Patience Principle

Most people fail because they are impatient. They give up too fast.They abandon their plan. They chase shortcuts. They panic when the journey is slow.

But the wealthy understand something:

Consistency outperforms intensity.

Time outperforms speed.

Wisdom outperforms luck.

If you learn this principle... you will win.

—-

◈ Generational Wealth

This is the highest level of financial growth.

It involves:

1. Teaching your children about money
2. Protecting assets legally
3. Building structures that outlive you

4. Creating family businesses
5. Documenting financial wisdom
6. Leaving a financial legacy

Generational wealth is not about inheritance alone — it is about transferring knowledge, values, and vision.

You become the turning point in your family story.

—-

◈ A Moment With You

Place your hand on your heart.

Close your eyes.

Whisper:

"I am building wealth brick by brick.

I am patient with my progress.

I am consistent with my habits.

My future is stable, strong, and abundant."

Your wealth does not need to arrive fast. It only needs to arrive surely.

⯑ Chapter 22 — The New You (Final Chapter)

"Your future is not waiting for luck — it's waiting for you."

This is the chapter where everything shifts. Not because the information changes — but because you do.

You've walked through mindset, discipline, skills, money habits, investing, relationships, growth, setbacks, and vision.

You've gained tools, strategies, and clarity. You've learned what it takes to build wealth — slowly, steadily, intentionally, spiritually.

Now it's time to step into the version of yourself who lives it.

This final chapter is not about money at all. It's about identity — who you become on the journey.

Because all the financial principles in the world mean nothing if you still see yourself as the old you.

—-

⯑ The Transformation Begins Within

Every lasting transformation begins in the heart. Before the numbers change...before the income grows... before the savings multiply... you must change first.

<u>You become:</u>

More focused
More disciplined
More intentional
More hopeful
More strategic
More confident
More courageous
More self-honoring
More spiritually aligned

Your habits change.
Your thinking changes.
Your expectations change.
Your boundaries change.
Your future changes.
You can't enter the next level with yesterday's mindset.

—-

◈ The New You Speaks Differently

The old you said:
"I can't save."
"I'm not good with money."
"I don't think I can succeed."
"I'm scared of taking risks."
"I don't deserve wealth."
"It's too late for me."
But the new you says:
"I can learn."
"I can grow."
"I am capable."
"I am disciplined."
"I respect my money."
"Wealth is my portion."
"I deserve abundance."
"My future is blessed."
"I am becoming better every day."
You speak life.
You speak power.
You speak vision.
Your words become your reality.

—-

◈ The New You Behaves Differently

Transformation is action.

The new you:

★ wakes up with purpose
★ tracks your money
★ plans your week
★ reads
★ learns
★ saves without excuses
★ invests without fear
★ spends with intention
★ cuts the unnecessary
★ protects your peace
★ chooses wise relationships
★ builds your future daily

This is not the version of you who reacts — this is the version of you who leads.

—-

◈ The New You Believes Differently

Everything you create flows from belief.

Believe:

★ That you deserve financial peace
★ That you can learn any skill
★ That God can multiply the work of your hands
★ That your steps are guided
★ That you are favored
★ That your hard work is not in vain

- ★ That your life can transform
- ★ That your family story can change with you

Belief doesn't remove challenges — it gives you strength to walk through them.

—-

◈ The New You Has Vision

You now understand wealth is not an event — it is a direction.

You are moving toward: stability, ownership, growth, investments, peace, legacy, generational change, freedom

Your vision becomes your compass. Your goals become your guardrails. Your habits become your vehicle. And slowly, beautifully, consistently — your future becomes real.

—-

◈ The New You Walks With God

This journey isn't powered by will alone —it is powered by grace.

God strengthens you.

God guides you.

God opens doors.

God gives wisdom.

God protects what you build.

God multiplies what you work for.

God aligns you with destiny.

You are not building alone.

You are building with divine partnership.

You are becoming who you were meant to be.

—-

◈ A Moment With You

Take a deep breath.

Place your hand on your chest.

Whisper softly:

"I am ready.

Ready to grow.

Ready to change.

Ready to rise.

Ready to build.

Ready to walk in wisdom.

Ready to become the version of myself

that wealth has been waiting for."

This is not the end of your story. This is the beginning of your elevation.

◈ You Are the New You Now

You are no longer reading information. You are stepping into transformation.

You are the person who: earns wisely, saves consistently, invests intentionally, dreams boldly, walks with purpose, builds with discipline, grows spiritually, rises continually

You are the turning point for your family.

You are the foundation of a new generation.

You are the one who breaks cycles and creates legacy.

You are the new you — and your new life begins now.

—-

◈ Final Page Closing Quote

"May your hands be guided, your steps be ordered, and your path be lit by the One who goes before you.

May your seeds multiply,your efforts bear fruit, and your faith draw favor from places you cannot see.

Walk boldly into your tomorrow — for Heaven has whispered your name into abundance."

Don't miss out!

Visit the website below and you can sign up to receive emails whenever Juliet Alambo publishes a new book. There's no charge and no obligation.

https://books2read.com/r/B-A-YGXQD-PYRRI

BOOKS 2 READ

Connecting independent readers to independent writers.

Did you love *Wealth Unleashed*? Then you should read *Praying Effectively*[1] by Juliet Alambo!

[2]

Are you tired of experiencing unanswered prayers? This book here is just for you. It will help you learn and discover the reasons behind all the hick ups in your prayer life. This book will open up the secrets behind effective prayer life and soon you will start experiencing and enjoying answers to prayers. Be blessed.

1. https://books2read.com/u/4D7YAD

2. https://books2read.com/u/4D7YAD

Also by Juliet Alambo

Ripples Of Faith
Hearts Of Valor (Ripples Of Faith)

Standalone
The Trouble Makers
Toto Gets Lost
God Is In My Story
The Rebel
Stepping Into God's Promises and Blessings
Deliverance In Christ Jesus
Beyond The Visible
Beauty With Character
Marriage With Purpose
Praying Effectively
Rosy The Lazy Girl
Atito The Foodious Boy
Life O Life
Merry Merry Christmas
Deep Trust In God
God's Grace To Man
Harry Visit's Grandma
Journeying Through Life

Money Matters
How To Have A Perfect Marriage
The Heiress Returns
Wealth Unleashed
Home This Christmas
Secret Sin
The Shivers Beneath
Christmas Healed Heart
The Star Of Christmas

About the Author

Juliet Alambo is an author, whose vision is to touch the hearts and the lives of her readers in a special way. Her works are inspired by her love for purity, holiness and righteousness in the Lord. She desires to see a people nurtured and groomed into responsible and God fearing people. She desires to see a morally upright society, a society and a people who love and respect each other and have high moral values and virtues. Juliet Alambo loves also to read and carry out research. And her beautiful and life changing moments is seeing the lives of her readers impacted positively through her works.

About the Publisher

Juliet Alambo is an author whose work is visioned towards touching and impacting the lives of her readers in a more deeper way. She envisions a people who are sharpened and shaped by her works into a God fearing and role models in the society. Juliet Alambo loves both researching, reading and writing books.

www.ingramcontent.com/pod-product-compliance
Lightning Source LLC
LaVergne TN
LVHW022036200926
848481LV00003B/708
* 9 7 9 8 2 3 1 0 2 1 3 6 9 *